The LITTLE BOOK of

Wild
Gardening

RHS The Little Book of Wild Gardening

Author: Holly Farrell

First published in Great Britain in 2022 by Mitchell Beazley,
a division of Octopus Publishing Group Ltd
Carmelite House, 50 Victoria Embankment, London EC4Y 0DZ
www.octopusbooks.co.uk

An Hachette UK Company

www.hachette.co.uk

Published in association with the Royal Horticultural Society

ISBN: 978-1-78472-833-5

A CIP record of this book is available from the British Library

Printed and bound in China

Conceived, designed and produced by The Bright Press
an imprint of The Quarto Group
The Old Brewery, 6 Blundell Street,
London N7 9BH, United Kingdom
T (0) 20 7700 6700
www.Quarto.com

Publisher: James Evans

Art Director: James Lawrence

Editorial Director: Isheeta Mustafi

Managing Editor: Jacqui Sayers

Project Editor: Katie Crous

Design: Wayne Blades

Illustrations: John Woodcock, Ellis Rose

Mitchell Beazley Publisher: Alison Starling

RHS Publisher: Rae Spencer-Jones

RHS Consultant Editors: Guy Barter, Simon Maughan

RHS Head of Editorial: Tom Howard

The Royal Horticultural Society is the UK's leading gardening charity
dedicated to advancing horticulture and promoting good gardening. Its charitable work
includes providing expert advice and information, training the next generation of gardeners,
creating hands-on opportunities for children to grow plants and conducting research into plants,
pests and environmental issues affecting gardeners.

For more information visit www.rhs.org.uk or call 0845 130 4646.

 RHS

The LITTLE BOOK of

Wild
Gardening

HOW TO WORK WITH NATURE TO CREATE
A BEAUTIFUL WILDLIFE HAVEN

MITCHELL BEAZLEY

CONTENTS

INTRODUCTION

Zoologist Dr Jennifer Owen is something of a legend among wildlife gardeners. Her suburban garden might be described as 'normal' in appearance; it doesn't set out to be a 'wildlife garden' and has a lawn, flowers and vegetables. From 1971 Owen recorded which creatures and plants she found over a 30-year period, admitting that she probably missed quite a few. She did note over 2,600 different species, of which 2,000 were insects. This represents a quarter of all known species in the UK.

A decade after Owen published her study, we are living in an age of a massive biodiversity crisis. All over the world, animal and insect species are in decline, their populations often falling at alarming rates or becoming extinct. Nearly 40 per cent of bee and hoverfly species are in decline across Europe, around 70 per cent of all UK butterfly species are in decline and as many as one-third of the USA's wildlife species are at increased risk of extinction. Everything is connected: we rely on insects for our own survival (not just for the pollination services they provide for our food crops), and the situation is both grim and urgent.

Creating a biodiverse haven for wildlife is easy. It obviously benefits the wildlife that will make a home in your garden, but it can also benefit you. The lockdowns during the Covid-19 pandemic brought us closer to the creatures living on our doorstep and reminded us of the power of the natural world. Creating a beautiful, sustainable garden (no matter its size)

generates an enormous sense of wellbeing and connection with nature, so isn't it time we found some space to share with wildlife?

If Jennifer Owen can find a quarter of all the UK's species in her garden without even specifically aiming to help wildlife, just think what a difference a few simple steps – a few more plants or a pond – could make. If we all do what we can to help the creatures with which we share this planet, together we can make a change for the better. All gardens can be beautiful, sustainable, productive and havens for wildlife: **all gardens can be wild gardens**.

A note on plant names

Throughout this book plants are referred to by their common names and their botanical Latin names. This is because common names vary widely and are not, unlike the botanical Latin name, unique to that plant. The exceptions are fruit and vegetable plants, which are referred to here solely by their common names unless particularly unusual. If there is no botanical Latin given then the Latin and common name are the same. Latin names of plants take the form of two parts: the first word is the genus, a subset of the family to which that plant belongs. The second word is the species name. Following that might be a particular cultivar (*culti*vated *vari*ety) that has been created by plant breeders.

For example:

Lavandula   *angustifolia*   'Hidcote'

↑   ↑   ↑

genus   species   cultivar

If a plant is referred to only by its genus name, it means that any plant of that genus would be suitable. Elsewhere there may be more particular species or even cultivar recommendations.

How to use this book

Chapter 1: Principles of Wild Gardening

This chapter outlines the key ideas behind creating a wildlife haven that is beautiful, practical and sustainable. It explains how to work with nature, debunks popular misconceptions of wild gardens and looks at the practicalities of making a vibrant ecosystem.

Chapter 2: The Wild Garden

Divided into sections about the different areas of the garden, in this chapter we look specifically at each area in turn: beds and borders; containers; trees, hedges and edges; lawns; edible gardens; and last but not least, how to incorporate wildlife-friendly water features into the garden.

Chapter 3: Helpful Habitats

Here we show various options for encouraging and hosting wildlife in your garden, whatever its size or type. From ways to add food sources to providing shelter and nesting opportunities, you can turn your garden space into a reserve for local nature.

Plant profiles

Included in chapters 2 and 3 are individual profiles of flowers, plants, vegetables and trees, all offering in-depth information on some of the best choices for what to grow in your wild garden space.

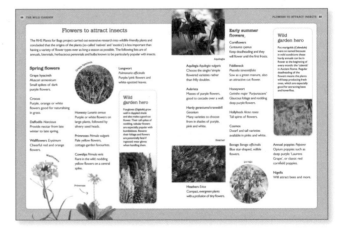

Finally, the book ends with a glossary, explaining technical terms, and a resources section including seed retailers, websites, books and other inspirational sources that will help you get going with growing your wild garden.

Viola,
see page 113

1

PRINCIPLES OF
WILD GARDENING

Unlike farms or public parks, a garden has to please no one but
its owner(s). It might be that the whole of the space is dedicated
to wilder habitats, but it can also be beautiful and productive
in the more traditional gardening senses. A wilder approach to
the garden is to simply create a space for the wildlife, to create
somewhere they will want to be. The more diverse the food and
shelter on offer, the more diverse your garden wildlife will be.
No matter the size or location of your garden, you can plant it so
that it will be attractive to insects, birds, frogs and slow worms.
If you don't have the space, time or inclination to incorporate
all the ideas in this book, creating a small wild garden will make
a big difference, especially as wildlife will use your garden
in conjunction with those of your neighbours and others
further afield.

WHAT IS WORKING WITH NATURE?

A wilder approach to the garden

Small changes in how we garden can make a big difference to wildlife. In a wild garden, the gardener works with nature rather than against her – in any case, it is a battle the gardener will never win, for Mother Nature is far mightier than us and will always have the last laugh. Inviting wildlife into the garden needn't mean a compromise on aesthetics – a border full of gorgeous flowers is ideal for pollinating insects – although it may prompt a reconsideration of the nature of beauty. Beauty is in the eye of the beholder after all, and a bee on a dandelion flower is arguably more beautiful than a patch of bare soil with no dandelion, and no bee.

What might a wilder approach look like?

A wild garden has a gardener that puts the needs of wildlife at the forefront of decision making.

For example:
...instead of a fence, choose a hedge;

...instead of spraying aphids with pesticides, leave them as food for ladybirds, hoverfly larvae and blue tits;

...instead of mowing the lawn, lie down on it and take a close-up look at the world under your feet. Don't mow it for a few weeks and you'll find yourself among clover and daisies, with the bumblebees and hoverflies enjoying it as much as you.

Wild gardening sees everything in the garden as part of the ecosystem and food chain. It means being patient and allowing nature to get on with things in her own way in places, but providing support and help in others. It means being forgiving if the lettuces are a bit nibbled, and allowing the blackbirds a few cherries as payment for the beauty of their songs.

Good for the gardener and the garden

By taking a step back, the gardener allows nature to take a step forward. Creating a space for wildlife helps to balance the garden ecosystem. A biodiverse garden with a stable ecosystem will be healthier and look after itself in many ways. Outbreaks of pests and diseases are minimised, because everything is kept in check within the food chain: pests are dealt with by their predators who are already resident in the garden. As a wild garden grows and matures, it becomes healthier; there is a compound growth of sustainable biodiversity.

The pollination cycle

Pollination is a beautiful cycle of mutual benefit. Flowers are pollinated by insects that visit to feed on the nectar and pollen; the insects also get pollen stuck to their bodies, transferring it to different flowers. This enables the flowers to set seed and so produce more flowers (and, therefore, food for insects) the following year. The gardener also benefits from the pollination of crops that provides fruit, vegetables, flowers and seeds.

A relaxed approach

Reducing or preferably eliminating the use of chemicals in the garden (pesticides, herbicides and/or weed killers and fertilisers) saves money and helps the health of the garden and the wider environment. Dense layers of planting minimise the need for weeding, and a more relaxed approach to 'weeds' saves effort and stress – see pages 18–19.

By letting go of our attempts to control all aspects of nature in our gardens we can relax and enjoy it more. By inviting wildlife in, we can foster a real connection with nature, which has enormous benefits for our mental wellbeing. A feeling of doing something to help the planet, of making a difference, is buoying in these days of climate and biodiversity crises. Finally, garden wildlife can be endlessly and enormously entertaining to watch.

Good for wildlife and the planet

Gardeners are in a unique position to help wildlife because they can create an artificially high number of micro-habitats within a single space. A farm, for instance, might have bountiful hedgerows, owl boxes and wildflowers, but they are all spread out over a large area. A wildlife garden – with a pond, flowers, long grass and a log pile, for example – can help a wealth of species all within a few square metres.

Evidence is emerging that some species are adapting to the supplementary food we provide in our gardens. Goldfinches now favour sunflower seeds over their more usual diet of nyger seeds, and great tits seem to be evolving to have longer beaks in the UK to take better advantage of garden bird feeders.

Ponds, flower borders and bird feeders bring gardens to life, creating spaces brimming with wildlife and wonder.

Wild gardens provide shelter and homes for species small and not-so-small whose habitats have been lost through urbanisation and intensive agriculture, thereby helping to protect against declines in their populations. Biodiversity, especially of insects, is key to the survival of our planet – and us. Each garden might be small, but it is part of a wider patchwork of gardens, and connected with the countryside, parks and other wild spaces. The more wild gardens that are created, the better and more biodiverse this living landscape will become.

There are other benefits to the planet, too. Growing plants locks in atmospheric carbon. Growing edible plants reduces food miles and the strain on worldwide resources from agriculture. Making more sustainable gardening choices (see pages 26–27) reduces the use of harmful chemicals and plastic.

Does wild mean weeds?

The short answer is an emphatic no! There is no fixed definition of what a weed *is* in any case – generally it is simply agreed that a weed is a plant in the wrong place. Thus self-seeding perennials and annuals causing a colour clash in a border would be as much weeds as docks and bindweed. Some weeds are, in another context, wildflowers (especially in lawns, see pages 94–95) or garden shrubs, such as buddleja. Many are also edible and/or have herbal health benefits, for example nettles, dandelions and chickweed.

To wildlife, however, there are no 'good' or 'bad' plants beyond those that do or don't supply them with the food they need. Many species benefit from a range of plants, and traditional 'weeds' need not form a part of a wild garden if you don't want them to. However, there are some species that do need particular plants and others that benefit from weeds in general. For example, red admiral and peacock butterflies lay their eggs on nettles (only when in a sunny patch though) so the caterpillars can eat the leaves when they hatch. Sycamore trees and herb robert are notorious for seeding everywhere, but their flowers are useful to bees and hoverflies.

A garden works best for wildlife when it is balanced and diverse in its plant offering. Some weeds may be extremely beneficial to wildlife, but a garden overrun with one or two types of weed is not going to be beneficial to a range of wildlife, just as a garden growing only lavender wouldn't be. The key is variety. Reclassifying some weeds to 'herbs' or 'wildflowers' and allowing them to grow in the garden can benefit wildlife and you, not least in that it means less weeding!

Buddleja is aptly commonly known as the butterfly bush

When weeds really are weeds

The traditional garden weeds have persisted down the generations for a reason: they have pernicious root systems and/or self-seed widely (although birds do enjoy the seeds sometimes too). Prevent them from taking too great a hold by digging up spreading roots and deadheading to prevent seeding.

Invasive plants, especially those that cause environmental problems such as Japanese knotweed and Himalayan balsam, should be removed as soon as possible and disposed of responsibly (check your local government website for help).

Prevent unwanted weeds from seeding

GARDENING WITH NATURE

All gardens can be wild gardens

No matter the size of your outdoor space — whether you've an acre or a window ledge — you can create a garden that will attract and help wildlife. Obviously the size and location of your space will determine to an extent the type of wildlife you'll see in your garden (don't expect hedgehogs on a fifth-floor balcony!) but the old saying 'build it and they will come' generally holds true.

A successful wild garden will provide food, water, shelter and somewhere to nest and breed for wildlife. Plants are fundamental, providing a large part of the food and shelter elements, to which can be added other features such as ponds and bird boxes. The greater the volume and variety of plants you can grow, the greater the range of wildlife you will be able to attract.

Food

Food might be nectar and pollen for insects, dead wood for beetles, or seeds and berries for birds. Grow plants that supply various types of food for as much of the year as possible, and consider putting out supplementary food (e.g. peanuts for birds).

Water

All creatures also need water to drink and wash safely. A bird bath, pond and/or bee drinker will be invaluable to them, especially in summer.

Shelter and a place to breed

Food and water will tempt visitors into your garden, but if you can also provide them with room to stay, they are more likely to make it their home. Bird boxes, ponds, log piles and compost heaps all create habitats. (Note that if birds and animals are raising families in your garden, they'll also need to be able to find enough food for their young, such as caterpillars and aphids for hungry chicks, and pond plants for tadpoles).

Design considerations

Whether you are planting a new garden from scratch or making small gradual changes to an existing garden, there are some factors to take into account when creating a wild garden. Generally, these all amount to the same idea: the less manmade and the more natural the garden, the friendlier it will be to wildlife. The more diverse habitats you can offer, the more wildlife you will be able to host in your garden.

Reduce paving

Wherever possible, use natural materials for paths and seating areas, such as grass, low-growing plants such as chamomile, or bark chippings. Use gravel rather than paving slabs if it's essential to have a path that is relatively dry to walk on at all times. See also 'Container gardens' (page 64), and 'Dry gardens' (page 62) for advice on making manmade features as wild as possible without removing them entirely.

Loose, natural paths will allow air to get to the soil and plant roots, and will provide natural corridors through which wildlife can travel.

Outdoor lighting

Artificial lighting wreaks havoc on nocturnal (and diurnal) wildlife, whose natural rhythms and navigational abilities are disrupted by it. If lighting paths or driveways is essential, use motion-sensor lights that come on only for a short time when needed. Candles are a more wildlife-friendly and atmospheric option for outdoor seating than bright fairy lights or spotlights.

Use natural materials

Choose wild lawns or gravel gardens instead of decking or Astroturf, which have little to zero benefit for wildlife or the environment, and can actually harm creatures (insects and invertebrates can drown on poorly drained Astroturf). Use natural timber from local tree surgeons or sawmills if possible, or reclaimed/recycled wood (but avoid those treated with potent chemicals). Drilling holes into wooden features creates space for solitary bees and wasps to lay eggs and other insects to shelter.

Wildlife-friendly garden maintenance

Helping wildlife in the garden is not just about what we plant, but also about how to look after it in a way that strikes a balance between aesthetics for the gardener and benefit for wildlife. The garden need not be messy or unkempt, but a few little changes here and there can make all the difference for wildlife, and make life easier for the gardener – you!

Garden practice

Birds can nest from spring to late summer, so don't cut hedges or shrubs during this time if possible. If you need to cut them, first check the hedge thoroughly for active nests. Composting garden waste, or building it into dead hedges and log piles (see pages 132–133), and regularly mulching the beds are all also easy tasks to incorporate into the gardening year that will make your garden both more sustainable and wildlife-friendly.

Flower borders

Encourage each plant to produce the most flowers it can over the spring and summer for a steady supply and good quantity of nectar and pollen. In spring, later-flowering plants such as Michaelmas daisies can be given the 'Chelsea chop', pruning off the top third of the stems at the time of the RHS Chelsea Flower Show in late May. This will extend their flowering season and encourage them to branch, which makes the stems less likely to flop. Upright flowers are more easily accessible for insects, and if they also have seed heads, they are accessible for birds too – stake tall herbaceous perennials if necessary.

Perennials that flower earlier can be cut back in July (the 'Hampton Hack', for the Hampton Court Flower Show) to encourage a second flush of flowers. Annuals and shrubs such as roses that will repeat flower can be deadheaded regularly to encourage a succession of flowers. If you are more concerned with providing late-season nectar, continue to deadhead into autumn. To save seed and/or provide seed heads for the birds, stop deadheading in late summer.

Worms are integral to a healthy soil

Don't be too tidy

Unless they are diseased (e.g. with rose blackspot), fallen leaves can be left on flowerbeds – the worms will munch them up. Leave herbaceous perennial stems standing over winter, as they can provide shelter among their stems for many creatures, such as ladybirds.

Gardening sustainably

The more plants you can squeeze into your garden, the more atmospheric carbon you will be able to capture and store in the soil. Other steps to reduce the impact your garden has on the environment generally means eschewing the garden centre and getting back to basics.

Reduce and reuse

By making your garden as self-sufficient as possible, using as few gardening products as you can, you can reduce the environmental implications of the transport and packaging of such products. Save seeds and divide herbaceous plants to expand your plant collection, swapping with friends or at community swaps if you have surplus or fancy growing something new.

When buying plants, source them from local nurseries, ideally buying bare root or wrapped in newspaper rather than plastic pots (ask to remove the pots at the till). Gravel and compost can be bought loose in bulk – share the load with a neighbour or the whole street! – to eliminate plastic sacks.

Biodegradable pots can be planted out in the soil with the seedlings; reused egg cartons make environmentally friendly seed trays.

Newspaper
seedling pots

Collect rain in a water butt for watering and make your own compost and fertiliser (see pages 40–41). If you need to buy fertiliser, look for organic plant-based ones such as seaweed feed. Grow a hazel or bamboo plant if you've the space, and cut stems for stakes and bean poles. New Zealand flax (*Phormium*) and nettle fibres can be used as biodegradable twine rather than buying string.

Recycle

If you do have plastic pots and sacks, reuse them until they perish (old sacks can be used to contain leafmould), then recycle. Most compost sacks are recyclable now, and even black plastic pots can be taken to recycling collection points at garden centres, or, if they're still usable, try leaving pots outside your property for other gardeners to take. Pots for seedlings can be made out of newspaper (there's a handy wooden tool called a paper potter that helps with this task) or cardboard (i.e. toilet roll tubes) for young plants or seedlings. Garden waste isn't really waste at all: it's ingredients for homemade compost.

New Zealand flax (*Phormium tenax*)

Vegan gardening

Homemade compost and fertilisers (see pages 40–41) avoid the use of animal products in the garden. Typically animal products are found in proprietary plant feeds (those based around blood, fish and bone being an obvious example) and also in some soil improvers and composts.

Wildlife corridors and connections

Your wild garden is not an island, but rather a piece of a larger patchwork of gardens, parks, verges, riverbanks and countryside in which wildlife finds a home. Being part of this patchwork means that you don't necessarily have to supply every possible habitat yourself: if your neighbour has a pond, you don't need one, but the wildlife that will live in its environs will use your garden too.

Pets in wild gardens

There's no two ways about it: cats are bad news for wildlife. They are known killers of birds, amphibians, reptiles and small mammals, including bats – and any aspiring wildlife gardener should think twice about getting a cat. If you already have one, keep them shut in at night. Bells on their collars may help, but the effectiveness of them in scaring off all wildlife in time before an attack is mixed.

The good news is dogs are generally not such a threat to wildlife, and that creating a wildflower lawn with lots of clover can benefit you and the bees: unlike grass, clover is immune to dog urine, so no more brown patches!

Look to your surroundings for inspiration on what sort of garden to create. You could provide similar habitats to those nearby to further help species known to be living and/or breeding there (consult your local wildlife groups for information) and/or provide different habitats to try and increase the local biodiversity.

For those creatures that can fly, accessing your garden within that wider landscape will be easy enough, but for those that crawl, hop, slither and snuffle, you will need to allow and/or create safe access points. Holes in the bottom of walls and fences, sheltered with plants to create a safe scurry-way, will connect your garden with neighbours' gardens and paths.

Protecting wildlife

Signs asking drivers to slow down for hedgehogs, frogs and toads are available if you live near a road.

Provide plants
for cover

Leave access
holes in fences

The garden ecosystem

A well-balanced ecosystem includes a myriad of food chains and webs, connecting the producers (plants), consumers (insects, birds and mammals) and decomposers (the animals, fungi and bacteria that turn waste matter into soil). The soil feeds the plants so the cycle can continue.

Climbers A gamut of habitats and food for wildlife on walls and fences.

Compost Provides plenty of insects for the birds and bats and a home for slow worms, if the heap is open.

Soil, mulch and leaf litter Will get eaten by detritivores such as slugs and turned into the soil by worms. Home to many food webs of its own, healthy soil is full of microscopic life.

Trees and shrubs Provide habitats, food and shelter for insects, birds and mammals. A single tree can support hundreds of different species. Varied layers of planting offer a range of habitats; flowers and berries provide food.

Flowers and grass Flowers in borders and lawns provide food for insects; extend nectar availability through the year with different annual and perennial blooms. Differing heights of grass provides a range of insect habitats and feeding opportunities for birds.

A helping hand

- Install nesting boxes and bug hotels to encourage wildlife to stop over and stay.
- Build connecting tunnels through gates, fences and walls to allow wildlife to come and go easily and link to the wider ecosystem.
- Add water – another style of habitat and somewhere for creatures to drink.

Creating and maintaining a healthy soil

Good soil is the literal and metaphorical foundation of gardening. Soil is home to billions of bacteria, fungi and other organisms – it is estimated a single teaspoon of healthy soil contains more living organisms than there are people on Earth – and it locks in atmospheric carbon. Putting some time into regenerating your soil and helping to keep it healthy will pay enormous dividends to not only your plants, but also to wildlife and the environment. No matter how bad or thin your soil at the moment, it can be improved easily in both the short and long term.

Take care of the soil

Treat the soil for what it is – a delicate ecosystem – and try not to physically disrupt it too much. Adopting a no-dig system (see page 104 and page 140) helps to minimise disturbance that can damage the soil organisms and webs of connections between them. Avoid treading on the soil where possible, especially when it is wet, as undue compaction reduces the aeration and therefore the health of the soil. Create narrow beds and/or use a plank to spread your weight when planting.

Feed the soil, not the plants

A dense planting scheme keeps the soil covered and prevents erosion by wind and water. Leaves and other dead plant matter from these plants will also get taken into the soil by worms and eaten by detritivores, so don't be too tidy. If a vegetable patch or other area of soil is going to be bare and empty for a while, sow a quick-maturing crop such as radishes or some green manure to keep it covered (see pages 104–105).

The wonder of mulch

A layer of mulch – which could be leafmould, compost, well-rotted horse manure or woodchip – sequesters carbon, protects against erosion and feeds the soil and its organisms. Apply it at least once a year in early spring and/or early winter to cover any bare soil, but avoid covering over plant shoots and getting too close to woody stems and trunks.

Soil management for wildlife

• Never use proprietary compost mixes containing peat, the creation of which will have destroyed peat bogs, which are invaluable carbon sinks and very slow-growing wildlife habitats. Carbon sinks absorb and store more carbon from the atmosphere than they release.

• Beetles and other creatures that need to get between soil and the open air will be trapped by sheets of weed-supressing plastic, old carpet and other solid barriers put over the soil, so avoid them if possible.

Choosing the right plant

The gardener's maxim 'right plant, right place' can preclude many a gardening disaster. Lavender, for example, evolved to grow in the thin, rocky soils and hot sun of the Mediterranean, and will die rather than thrive if planted in a shady, boggy spot.

How to know what to plant

The RHS website gives the ideal growing conditions in profiles of thousands of plants and has a searchable database of plants for specific planting situations (see page 140).

Visiting gardens in the local area can also provide inspiration – make a note of what is growing well and plants you like. Observe, too, how the plants already in your garden are performing, and don't be afraid to move a plant to a better spot.

Plants for Pollinators

The Plants for Pollinators list is managed by the RHS and includes hundreds of plants known to be especially valuable to wildlife, especially bees and other pollinators. See the RHS website for the full list.

← Lavender has both pollen and nectar to feed bees

Check plant labels for guidance, and ask the staff at plant nurseries for advice on their plants.

Look at the plant itself for clues: are the leaves adapted to prevent water loss (e.g. small, thin, oily, hairy, waxy and/or silvery), like rosemary? If so, the plant has evolved in hot, dry climes and should be planted in full sun. On the other hand, the wide green leaves of hostas, for example, are adapted to absorb the most sun they can, indicating they have evolved to grow in dappled shade.

Should we only plant native species?

The whole concept of 'native' plants is fraught with difficulties. Its meaning is varied and arbitrary across the world. When do you draw the line in history after which a plant could be considered native – before the introductions of the plant hunters in the nineteenth century, for example, or when the continents finally split apart from each other over 200 million years ago? So long as a plant grows well in your garden and has some value for wildlife, its origins are neither here nor there.

Successful planting

Having chosen suitable plants for your garden, it then pays to take note of a few simple measures to ensure they will get off to a good start in your garden. Successful planting avoids the disappointment of losing plants and wasting money.

How to plant

Make sure the hole is big enough! The top of the root ball should not protrude above soil level, and bare tree or shrub roots should not be bent around to fit in the hole. The hole does not need to be deeper than the roots or root ball, but should be at least as wide. Remove any large stones from the backfill; you can mix a little garden compost in with the backfill soil, but it is not essential.

When to plant

Autumn and spring are the best seasons to put in new plants in the garden, although bare-root trees and shrubs can be planted from late autumn to late winter when they are available. The soil is warm and there is usually sufficient rainfall to help the new plants get established before either winter dormancy or summer growth. Avoid planting when frosts are forecast or into frozen, very wet or dry soil.

Put bare-root plants into the ground as soon as possible after buying or taking delivery of them, but plunge their roots in a bucket of water for around 2 hours beforehand.

Root check

Take plants out of their pots before buying if possible to check they have a well-developed root system like the one above. Too few roots indicate the plant has only recently been potted on and doesn't offer value for money. If too many roots are wrapped around one another ('rootbound'), the roots will take longer to branch out into the surrounding soil once planted.

Sustainable water in the garden

Water is a limited resource, and minimising our use of it helps the wider environment. If possible, collect rainwater for use in the garden and especially ponds. Over time, watering with tap water can raise the pH of the soil in hard-water areas.

Reducing the need for water

Choose the right plant for the location and soil (see pages 34–35) so they are suited to the available water levels, and choose perennials instead of thirsty annuals. Put new plants in the ground in autumn rather than spring, so they have plenty of time to establish their roots before summer and the weather can provide the water they need at this time. An annual mulch of compost or other organic matter (in spring, autumn or both) can help preserve soil moisture, but don't make it too thick or it'll be impenetrable for beetles.

Where possible, plant in the ground rather than in containers, and if pots are your only option, use the biggest ones possible so they can hold more water. Water before the sun is too hot in the early morning to minimise waste through evaporation (the evening is also fine, but damp ground overnight encourages slugs and snails), and always direct the water at the ground and/or compost, not the foliage.

If watering or topping up ponds, use a water butt and a watering can rather than a hose, to encourage mindful use of water.

Installing a water butt

The best spot for a water butt is somewhere that's easy to access but that's out of the way, under a drainpipe from a house or shed roof, for example. To prevent it from overflowing in heavy rain, use a diverter kit (available from homeware/DIY stores). These direct the rain into the butt until it is full, then send the rest down the drain. If you've the space, connect further water butts to the first one so they also get filled in heavy downpours.

It's best if the butt has a (child-safe) lid to prevent midges breeding in it and insects or birds drowning.

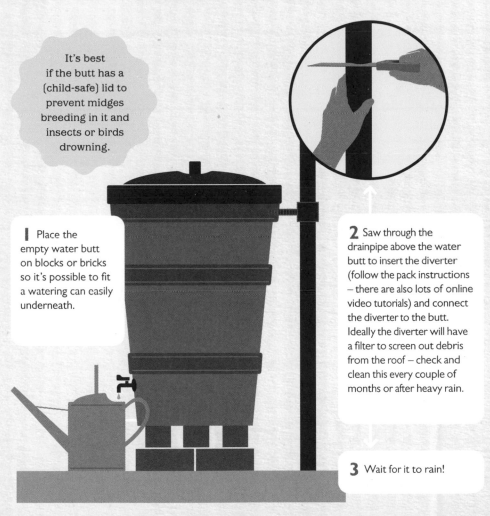

1 Place the empty water butt on blocks or bricks so it's possible to fit a watering can easily underneath.

2 Saw through the drainpipe above the water butt to insert the diverter (follow the pack instructions – there are also lots of online video tutorials) and connect the diverter to the butt. Ideally the diverter will have a filter to screen out debris from the roof – check and clean this every couple of months or after heavy rain.

3 Wait for it to rain!

Composting

Composting household and garden waste reduces landfill rubbish, produces a rich and fertile mulch, and locks in carbon. With compost bins for all sizes and types of garden, everyone can create their own 'black gold'. Keep a roughly equal balance between green/wet and brown/dry ingredients in the compost bin. Chopping into small pieces speeds up the rotting process, and turn compost (mix it up) regularly.

 Dampen open heaps of compost and leafmould in dry weather

Don't add: cooked food waste, oils/fats, meat/fish, dairy products, cat/dog poo. Biodegradable plastic substitutes can take a long time to rot in domestic heaps.

Kill roots of pernicious weeds (e.g. bindweed, horsetail) before composting by drowning them in a bucket for a month.

Good browns: thin woody prunings (put bigger bits into a dead hedge, see page 133), dry leaves, dead plant stalks, cardboard and paper, 100 per cent cotton or wool clothes, pet and human hair, wood shavings (e.g. hamster bedding).

Good greens: grass clippings, weeds and other plant material, kitchen scraps/peelings.

Making leafmould

Autumn leaves composted separately produce leafmould, a moisture-retentive organic matter ideal for mulching (after one year) or using as seed compost (after two years). Gather the leaves into an open wire bin or stuff them into old compost bags or sacks, pierced to allow air flow, and leave to rot.

Wild garden hero: Comfrey

Plants can be given a little boost by watering them with homemade comfrey fertiliser. It can be invasive, so plant the sterile variety *Symphytum officinale* 'Bocking 14', which will still flower for the bees. To make the feed, simply submerge a bucketful of leaves in water for around a month (covered to safeguard wildlife, plus it's pretty smelly). Strain off the liquid and water onto plants undiluted; compost the rotted leaves.

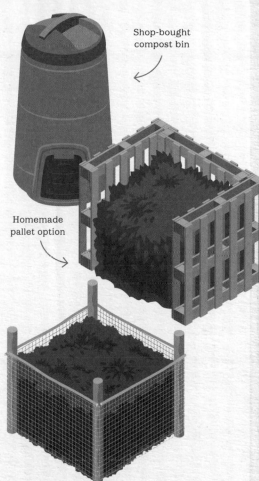

Shop-bought compost bin

Homemade pallet option

Homemade with wire and posts

When adding spent compost from pots, check for, remove and relocate glistening, spherical slug eggs and C-shaped vine weevil grubs (white with a brown head).

Put the heap directly on the ground to allow worms to move up into it. If you need an enclosed system (e.g. on a balcony) it's still worth making compost.

Open-top heaps attract birds and bats to eat the flying bugs that live off the heap.

A healthy heap will be teeming with detritivores such as slugs and snails, worms, woodlice, beetles and springtails.

Take care when turning or emptying compost not to hurt any wildlife enjoying its humid warmth (and feasting on the detritivores) such as amphibians, slow worms and snakes, who may also lay eggs in the heap.

Wildlife-friendly pest and disease maintenance

Even in the most diverse wild garden with plenty of pest predators, companion plants and healthy soil, edible crops and ornamentals can still sometimes be affected by caterpillars, slugs, aphids and many other beasts large and small. Before stepping out to do battle, consider if the wildlife is even a pest at all.

Any kind of pesticides are best avoided, even the organic ones, as they are still toxic and can have unintended consequences in the wider ecosystem. Be patient, too – although there can be a slight time lag after a particular bug population rises, predators will move in. The predators need something to eat, so it's necessary to tolerate a small population of the pests and their prey to encourage them.

Deterrents

Simply being in a (kitchen) garden frequently will ensure the wildlife keeps to the shadows – or try a scarecrow or old CDs hung from a branch. Resistant varieties of crops can be useful, such as 'Flyaway' for carrot root fly and 'Sarpo Axona' for potato blight, or sow early or late to avoid when pests are most prevalent. Befuddle pests by mixing crops together (see page 111).

For every squashed caterpillar, that's one less butterfly or one less meal for a blue tit chick

Use well-secured physical barriers of fine mesh to keep insects off vegetables and birds off fruit only if considered really necessary, especially as these are inevitably made from plastic. Birds, bats, amphibians and reptiles are more likely to be ensnared in larger netting holes. Bags/sleeves for single branches/small trees are better choices; fruit trees trained against a wall are easier to net than free-standing specimens.

Prevention and other measures

- Clear away infected plant material and snip off infected stems promptly.
- Disinfect gardening tools between uses.
- Rotate crops to avoid a build-up of pests and diseases ready to reinfect the same crop next year.
- Nematodes (microscopic predators and parasites) for slugs and vine weevil can be ordered online and watered onto the soil, but should only be used to target specific areas and as a last resort.
- Be vigilant and remove pests perceived as a problem. Aphids are easily squashed, slugs and snails can be relocated (take them at least 20m/22yd away, to somewhere there will be predators, such as a local park or scrubland).

Beware homemade remedies

Homemade sprays, using ingredients such as garlic, chillies and washing-up liquid, may have some effect on pests such as aphids, snails and slugs, but their wider effect on the ecosystem is still unknown and they can damage the plants themselves.

Garden wildlife to spot

The wildlife you are likely to spot in your garden depends on what is able to come there – how accessible your garden is and what lives locally – and the type of garden you have. All types of creatures, great and small, might come to enjoy your garden; enjoy sharing it with them.

Snakes Grass snakes are the species most commonly found in gardens, usually in compost heaps or ponds. They're harmless to people, eating mainly amphibians, fish and small birds.

Starlings

Birds Common species include blue tits, sparrows, finches, robins, blackbirds, starlings, thrushes, pigeons and corvids (crows, rooks and ravens), plus birds of prey such as falcons and owls.

Frogs and toads Frogs have smooth skins and brighter colouring than larger, warty toads. Both enjoy a diet of slugs, snails and flies. Habitat loss and disease has led to a widespread population decline.

The harmless grass snake

Slow worms This harmless, legless lizard is a reptile but not a snake, or a worm! Often preyed upon by cats and in a general population decline, it eats invertebrates such as slugs.

Newts Amphibious predators, also in decline, of slugs and other land and water invertebrates. Subject to habitat protection in some countries.

A smooth, or 'common', newt

Slow worm

Find lizards in sunny spots

Shrew

Lizards Common lizards like to bask
and hunt (spiders and insects) in warm
spots such as walls and piles of stones
or long grass.

Hedgehogs Bumbling hedgehogs eat
beetles, earwigs, slugs, worms and caterpillars,
roaming widely each night to find them and
hibernating in winter.

Mice, shrews and voles Hard to spot
in gardens – more likely you'll see evidence
of their presence, such as missing seeds
or nibbled bulbs, but they don't cause
extensive damage.

Foxes and badgers Nocturnal, although
urban foxes are often also seen in daytime.
If they are determined to visit, it can be hard
to stop them. Badgers eat mainly worms, but
also predate on hedgehogs. Foxes will eat
more or less anything they can find.

Hedgehog

Badgers are usually shy of people

Bees and bumblebees There are over 250 species of bee in the UK. Aside from the honeybee, and 25 types of bumblebee, the remainder are solitary bees, including leafcutter, mason, wool carder and hairy-footed flower bees. All feed on nectar and pollen.

Hoverflies Striped to resemble bees and wasps (to deter predators), hoverflies do not sting and are one of the gardener's best friends. The adults feed on nectar, particularly from daisy and umbelliferous flowers, but the larvae are voracious carnivores, munching through hundreds of aphids before pupating.

A hoverfly enjoying daisies

Ladybirds eat common pests

Ladybirds Can have between 2 and 24 spots, sometimes stripes, and are not always red and black. They eat aphids both as adults and larvae. Harlequin ladybirds, introduced to Europe and the USA as biological pest controls, also prefer aphids but can eat butterfly and moth eggs and other species. Research is continuing on the effects of the harlequins on our ecosystems.

Butterflies Have suffered an extreme decline in their numbers in the last 50 years. Providing both flowers for the adults and food plants for their caterpillars can help bring these beautiful insects to our gardens.

Moths Some species – such as the cinnabar, garden tiger and elephant hawk moth – are extremely striking as adults and caterpillars. Many particularly favour wildflowers.

The beautifully coloured cistus forester moth

A white admiral on sedum

Wasps and hornets Social, solitary and parasitic wasps and hornets are all prey to birds and only aggressive if attacked. They eat aphids, caterpillars and other insects, and help to clear up fallen fruit.

Hornet

Crane fly

Black ants

Crane fly/daddy longlegs Around 300 species of crane flies exist in the UK alone. Adults, characterised by their gangly legs and long wings, appear in late summer. The larvae (known as leatherjackets) eat the roots of grass.

Shield bugs have piercing sucking mouthparts

Ants Although they can improve the soil structure around a colony, their main wildlife benefit (unfortunately for them) is as prey for other insects and birds.

Shield bugs So-named for their shield-shaped body, these bugs can be a variety of colours depending on their species. They eat plant sap. The southern green shield bug and brown marmorated stink bug can be problematic.

Aphids The bug gardeners love to hate, greenfly and blackfly and many other species in between are food for so many other types of wildlife that they are worth tolerating.

A ladybird feasts on blackfly

Beetle

Moles are most active in late winter and early spring

Beetles Unsung garden heroes, beetles are the largest insect family and in severe general decline. Some are pollinators, some predators and some detritivores; create diverse habitats to accommodate them.

Squirrels The grey species, not the rarer, less destructive red, is likely to be the one trying to get to the peanuts in your bird feeder. Birds of prey and pine martens will take young squirrels (kittens) and adults.

Moles Need deep soil to tunnel for food: earthworms, and soil grubs including carrot root fly. Their tunnels aid drainage and soil aeration. Molehills can be raked smooth again; the moles themselves are prey for owls, buzzards and stoats.

The grey squirrel is an agile climber

Two young wild rabbits

Rabbits and hares Rabbits can do a lot of damage in productive and ornamental gardens and breed like, well, rabbits. However, 90 per cent of rabbits die within a year of being born, and both young and adults are important prey for larger mammals and birds of prey. Hares prefer eating grass and are less common.

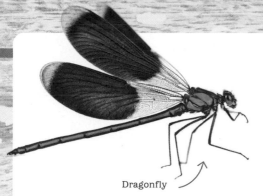

Dragonfly

Pond invertebrates Water boatmen, pond skaters, damselflies and dragonflies could all visit a garden pond, as well as other wildlife such as water snails and water spiders, all working within its own ecosystem.

Invertebrates The minibeasts under logs and fallen leaves, many are detritivores, such as slugs, snails, centipedes, millipedes, earwigs, woodlice and worms. They help keep the soil healthy and turn dead plants into food for the living ones.

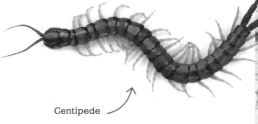

Centipede

Grasshoppers Chirping grasshoppers and crickets (the latter have antennae longer than their body, the former shorter) eat long grass and 'sing' to attract a mate.

Bats There are more than 1,400 species of bat in the world. Habitat loss, urbanisation, cat attacks and night lighting have led to population decline. Bats in a garden proves the area is a rich and diverse habitat.

← Grasshopper

Greater horseshoe bat

Spiders Well-known eaters of flies, spiders are an essential part of a healthy ecosystem.

Garden spider

2

THE WILD GARDEN

Plants are the basis of all life in a wild garden. Fill your space with as many plants as you can and you will create a haven of food and shelter for all manner of wildlife, from tiny bugs to squat toads, cheeky robins to snuffling hedgehogs – and everything in between. Creating a wildlife-friendly oasis doesn't happen overnight, and often it's easier to make changes to the garden in stages, taking each area and element in turn. Every change will help bring more wildlife into your garden – and help you to enjoy your garden space more and more.

BEDS AND BORDERS
Planting for year-round nectar

In a wild garden, some plants are more valuable than others: the more nectar and pollen a flowering plant can provide, the more wildlife it will benefit. Bumblebees, honey and solitary bees, butterflies, wasps, hoverflies, beetles, moths, true bugs and more all need flowers in order to help pollinate our crops of fruit and vegetables. The insects, in turn, are a meal for the rest of the food chain above them.

Leguminous flowers (from the pea/bean family) have high-quality pollen, so a wigwam of runner beans or sweet peas can provide bounty for both you and the bees

Less predictable seasons mean that some species — insects and invertebrates included — may not hibernate as they need to. When they are active in the cold they need more food, so try to offer nectar and pollen all year round.

Continuous nectar supply

By using a variety of flowering plants it is easier to provide a continuous buffet of nectar and pollen. Herbaceous perennials and annuals flower in late spring, summer and autumn, but by adding flowering shrubs and bulbs or biennials, your garden will have flowers in winter and early spring as well. Choosing plants that give value for space — those that flower all season long, such as salvias and Erysimum 'Bowles's Mauve', and trees that provide prolific flowers — makes each patch work hard for its wildlife. See pages 54–57 for suggestions on nectar-rich flowers for all seasons.

Other ways to help pollinators

It can also help to consider the type of flowers on offer for bees and other wildlife. Single flowers — those with an open centre, such as daisies — provide nectar and pollen easily accessed by the insects. Double and

Umbelliferous flowers such as fennel (*Foeniculum vulgare*) and *Verbena bonariensis* are popular with hoverflies and butterflies, which use the large flower heads as landing pads

White flowers like this honesty (*Lunaria annua*) are visible at night, and so are popular with moths

frilly flowers, bred with ornamental appeal or novelty factor in mind, have often lost their nectaries and pollen-bearing anthers in favour of petals during the breeding process, and hold little value for wildlife. The more different shapes, colours and scents of flowers you are able to offer, the more insects you will attract, some of which have evolved mouth parts to be able to feed only on certain flowers.

Flowers to attract insects

The RHS Plants for Bugs project carried out extensive research into wildlife-friendly plants and concluded that the origins of the plants (so-called 'natives' and 'exotics') is less important than having a variety of flower types over as long a season as possible. The following lists are of annuals, biennials, herbaceous perennials and bulbs known to be particularly popular with insects.

Spring flowers

Grape hyacinth
Muscari armenicum
Small spikes of dark purple flowers.

Crocus
Purple, orange or white flowers good for naturalising in grass.

Daffodils *Narcissus*
Provide nectar from late winter to late spring.

Wallflowers *Erysimum*
Cheerful red and orange flowers.

Grape hyacinth

Honesty *Lunaria annua*
Purple or white flowers on large plants, followed by silvery seed heads.

Primroses *Primula vulgaris*
Pale yellow flowers, cottage-garden favourites.

Cowslips *Primula veris*
Rare in the wild; nodding yellow flowers on a central spike.

Lungwort
Pulmonaria officinalis
Purple/pink flowers and white-spotted leaves.

Wild garden hero

Foxgloves (*Digitalis*) grow well in dappled shade and also make a good cut flower. Their tall spikes of nodding, tubular flowers are especially popular with bumblebees. Beware: their foliage and flowers are potentially fatal if ingested; wear gloves when handling them.

Wallflowers

Primrose

Aquilegia

Aquilegia *Aquilegia vulgaris*
Choose the single/simple flowered varieties rather than frilly doubles.

Aubretia
Masses of purple flowers, good to cascade over a wall.

Hardy geraniums/cranesbill
Geranium
Many varieties to choose from in shades of purple, pink and white.

Heather

Heathers *Erica*
Compact, evergreen plants with a profusion of tiny flowers.

Early summer flowers

Cornflowers
Centaurea cyanus
Keep deadheading and they will flower until the first frosts.

Fiddleneck
Phacelia tanacetifolia
Sow as a green manure, also an attractive cut flower.

Honeywort
Cerinthe major 'Purpurascens'
Glaucous foliage and nodding deep purple flowers.

Hollyhock *Alcea rosea*
Tall spires of flowers.

Cosmos
Dwarf and tall varieties available in pinks and white.

Borage *Borago officinalis*
Blue star-shaped, edible flowers.

Borage

Wild garden hero

Pot marigolds (*Calendula*) were so named because in mild conditions these hardy annuals can be in flower at the beginning of every month: the 'calends' in Ancient Rome. Regular deadheading of the flowers means the plants will keep producing fresh ones, which are especially good for attracting bees and hoverflies.

Annual poppies *Papaver*
Opium poppies such as deep purple 'Laurens Grape', or classic red cornfield poppies.

Nigella
Will attract bees and more.

Angelica
A statuesque biennial/short-lived perennial.

Blooming angelica in summer

Evening primrose
Oenothera biennis
Biennial, bowl-shaped yellow flowers on tall stems.

Hyssop *Hyssopus officinalis*
Low-growing aromatic herb.

Hyssop

Comfrey *Symphytum*
The leaves can be used to make garden fertiliser.

Common comfrey

Valerian *Centranthus ruber*, *Valeriana officinalis*
Wide flower heads suit many pollinators.

Yarrows *Achillea*
Umbelliferous flowers and feathery foliage.

Common yarrow

Fleabane
Erigeron karvinskinansus
Suits naturalising in paving cracks or growing in pots.

Masterwort *Astrantia*
Compact mound of foliage and pincushion-shaped flowers.

Wild garden hero

Nepeta species flower for a long period, and cutting them back after flowering can induce a second flush of flowers later in the season. The variety 'Six Hills Giant' is especially popular with bumblebees, but for a smaller plant try 'Walker's Low'.

Lamiaceae family
Including herbs and lamb's ear (*Stachys byzantina*) Square stems; especially popular with pollinators.

Bellflower *Campanula*
Bumblebees love to buzz up into the nodding flowers.

Astrantia 'Roma'

Bellflower

Late summer flowers

Echinacea
Echinacea purpurea
Cone-shaped flowers; seed heads also popular with birds.

Single-flowered dahlia
Bold colours and repeat flowering if deadheaded.

Dahlia

Sunflower *Helianthus annuus*
Dwarf varieties and other colours available – they're not just tall and yellow!

Coneflower or black-eyed Susan *Rudbeckia*
Yellow flowers into autumn.

Turkish sage *Phlomis*
Whorls of flowers followed by seed heads popular with birds.

Sage *Salvia*
Both the edible herb and the ornamental varieties are popular with insects.

Verbena
Narrow stems and small flowerheads go well with grasses.

Autumn flowers

Autumn-flowering crocus or cyclamen
Pretty pink cyclamen or purple crocus contrast with autumn leaves.

Actaea simplex
Spikes of white, fragrant flowers; the Atropurpurea Group has purple foliage.

Japanese anemones
Anemone x hybrida
White or pink open flowers suit planting in drifts.

Japanese anemone

Sedums/ice plant
Hylotelephium spectabile
Large flat flowerheads on fleshy stems; Chelsea chop to avoid them flopping.

Wild garden hero

Michaelmas daisies (previously known as *Aster*, now classified as *Symphyotrichum* species) produce a mass of small daisy flowers in autumn. Cutting back the stems in late spring (see page 25) induces them to branch further and produce even more flowers.

Winter flowers

Snowdrops *Galanthus nivalis*
Iconic nodding white flowers of winter.

Winter aconite
Eranthis hyemalis
Yellow flowers good for hedgerows and under trees.

Hellebores
Helleborus
Bumblebees will hang upside down on these pastel flowers.

Flowers to grow for birds

In a flower border birds are primarily looking for food, which will either be from the plants — seeds, berries and buds — or from the insects which are themselves feeding on the plants. An infestation of caterpillars or aphids can often be dealt with swiftly by a flock of blue tits with hungry chicks to feed. Flower borders can also provide nesting material, such as twigs and the fluffy seed heads of old man's beard (*Clematis vitalba*).

As well as the plants listed below, which produce seeds popular with birds, any of the seed/nut or berry-bearing shrubs, trees and climbers (pages 78–81) would be good choices of food and shelter for birds in a wild garden.

Lavender *Lavandula*
Delay cutting back the flower spikes until the seeds have dropped.

Sunflower *Helianthus annuus*
If large seed heads start to droop, they can be cut off at the stem and hung upside down from a tree as a homegrown bird feeder.

The majestic sunflower

Lemon balm
Melissa officinalis
Fragrant herbaceous perennial also popular with bees; provides plentiful seeds.

Greater knapweed
Centaurea scabiosa
Pretty purple flowers similar to cornflowers; ideal for a perennial wildflower meadow.

Lemon balm (left)

Greater knapweed (right)

Dandelion
Taraxacum officinale
Useful plant for wildlife and humans, it deserves a better reputation; birds feed on insects on the plant and its seeds.

Verbena

Thistles
Carduus and *Cirsium*
Ornamental species of thistles are available, and edible cardoons, all of which attract birds with their rich sources of insect and seeds.

Nettle *Urtica dioica*
Birds love nettle seeds, and also pick off the caterpillars of the butterfly species that lay their eggs there.

Vervain
Verbena bonariensis
Tall, slender stems bear purple flowers late into autumn, followed by seeds for the birds.

Thistles

Devil's bit scabious
Succisa pratensis
Wildflower with flowers like purple pincushions; popular with butterflies (including the rare March fritillary butterfly) and moths; provides insect food as well as seeds for birds.

Wild garden hero

Birds, especially finches, balanced precariously on the tall seed heads of teasel plants (*Dipsacus fullonum*) is a lovely sight in autumn and winter. Empty seed heads can be cut down and sprinkled with bought seed before hanging in tree branches as extra food. The biennial plants suit a wildflower meadow or the back of a border.

Scabious flowers

Wildlife-friendly shrubs

Blossom, berry, seed and shelter

Although they might not be as pretty or exciting as herbaceous and annual flowers, shrubs form an essential part of a wild garden and are relatively low maintenance. Their woody stems and branching structures provide perching and even nesting sites for birds. Flowering shrubs are good for insects (and those that feed on the insects), and the subsequent berries and seeds provide food for birds. Their leaves are shelter and food for detritivores, and underneath you may even find amphibians, reptiles and small mammals making a home or simply using the shrubs as cover for moving about the garden.

> Some of those listed as good for hedges (see pages 84–87), such as *Viburnum* and *Sarcococca confuse*, would also work in a border setting.

KEY

....

✿ flowers
🍒 berries
❀ deciduous
🌿 evergreen

Butterfly bush *Buddleja*
✿ ❀

California lilac
Ceanothus
✿ 🌿

California lilac

Daphne
✿ ❀/🌿

Thorny olive, spiny oleaster, silverthorn
Elaeagnus
✿ 🌿   Thorny olive

Strawberry tree
Arbutus unedo
✿ 🍒 ❀

Cotoneaster
✿ 🍒 🌿

Japanese quince
Chaenomeles speciosa
✿ B 🌿

Japanese
quince

Spindle
Euonymus europaeus
✿ 🍒 ❀

Guelder rose
Viburnum opulus
✿ 🍒 ❀

Laburnum
✿ ❀

Laburnum

Lilac
❀ ✿

Magnolia

Magnolia
❀ ✿/🍃

Oregon grape
Mahonia aquifolium
❀ 🍒 🍃

Firethorn
Pyracantha
❀ 🍒 🍃

Rhododendron
❀ 🍃

Firethorn

Flowering currant *Ribes*
❀ 🍒 ✿

Japanese spirea

Snowberry *Symphoricarpos albus*
🍒 ✿

Spirea *Spirea japonica*
❀ ✿

Winter honeysuckle
Lonicera fragrantissima
and *L. x purpusii*
❀ ✿

Wild garden hero

Elder (*Sambucus nigra*) is a forager's favourite for its perfumed flowers and immune-boosting berries, both of which are used to make drinks. Elder is also a favourite with wildlife. In spring the huge flower heads are visited by many insects, ensuring a crop of dark purple berries in the early autumn that are popular with birds (which, unlike humans, can eat the berries raw). The hollow dead stems of elder are also used as nesting and overwintering places by various insects and invertebrates.

Ribes

Roses,
especially species roses
Rosa
❀ ✿

Dry gardens

Dry or gravel gardens are low-maintenance borders created on particularly fast-draining, sandy or rubble-filled soil. They require drought-resistant plants that are adapted to these conditions, and suit many Mediterranean herbs, ornamental grasses and other shrubs and perennials. When used in place of impermeable tarmac or paving, they not only add wildlife-friendly plants, but also help to reduce rain run-off that contributes to flooding.

Bees, butterflies, hoverflies and other pollinators will visit flowering plants and enjoy a moment's basking on the warm stones, and you may even spot a lizard enjoying the sunshine too. Spiders, predatory insects and invertebrates and birds will predate on them and find plenty of dry shelter among the bases of plants, especially tufty grasses. Birds may also help themselves to fluffy grasses and seed heads to make their nests, as well as feeding on the insects.

Planting a gravel garden

Hot, sunny corners and front gardens are particularly suited to this style of planting. As gravel can be used to cover a whole area, paths, seating and even driveways can be incorporated into the garden, while the plants flow seamlessly through it in drifts. Planting in groups of at least three plants of the same species and repeating the same plant through several locations in the garden helps to tie the design together.

One cubic metre of gravel will cover around 20m² (215 sq ft) in a 5cm- (2in-) thick layer. Source reclaimed or recycled ceramic gravel if possible, or ensure new gravel has not been dredged from the seabed (which seriously damages marine wildlife ecosystems). Avoid using a weed-suppressing plastic membrane as it acts as a barrier to beetles and other creatures wanting to move between soil and the open air.

Ideal plants for a dry garden

Flowering oregano

Yarrow *Achillea*
Varieties offer flowers in
pink, white, yellow and red.

Lavender *Lavandula*
Fragrant glaucous foliage and
purple spikes of flowers.

Sea holly and sea kale
Erynigium and
Crambe maritima
Coastal plants.

Eryngium

Oregano/marjoram
Origanum vulgare
Small pink/purple flowers
above sprawling foliage.

Lavender

Thyme *Thymus*
Compact plants produce
a mass of tiny flowers.

**Feather grass, fountain
grass and elephant grass**
Stipa, *Pennisetum* and
Miscanthus
Ornamental grasses.

Annual poppies
Papaver and
Eschscholzia californica
Will happily self-seed around
the garden once established.

Rosemary *Salvia rosmarinus*
Evergreen, woody plant
with blue flowers in spring.

Chamomile *Chamaemelum*
Low-growing foliage and
daisy-like flowers.

**Catmint, globe thistle
and red hot pokers**
Nepeta, *Echinops* and
Kniphofia
Herbaceous perennials.

Red hot poker

Chamomile

CONTAINER GARDENS
Wildlife in small spaces

Natural grassland is an important carbon sink, locking away atmospheric carbon almost as effectively as trees. A lawn is more wildlife-friendly than paving, decking or Astroturf, and with a few simple tweaks you can create a beautiful lawn-based habitat.

Offer food

Flowering and fruiting plants will bring in insects, while invertebrates and perhaps toads, lizards and other creatures will scurry around the bottom of pots (take care when moving them). Where there is prey for them, birds will come too, but adding bird feeders will be an extra draw.

Over the last few decades the soil in our back gardens and especially front gardens has been disappearing under concrete, paving stones and decking. In this and other situations – such as rented accommodation and urban living – where it's often not possible to remove paving and/or there are smaller outdoor spaces to work with, there is still a lot that can be done to make the area wilder, no matter how small it is.

Green the grey

Planting, rather than paving and other hard surfaces, helps to keep gardens cool in the summer heat, lessen rain run off that can lead to flooding, traps air and noise pollution, is more wildlife-friendly and improves our mental wellbeing.

Where there is no soil, pots, large planters and raised beds can be used to grow plants. Trailing plants can be suspended in hanging baskets or from window boxes. In small gardens, make

each plant really work for its space by choosing species with a long flowering season or those that offer both flowers and fruit (or an edible element for you).

If it is possible to lift some paving slabs you can use the reclaimed space to grow climbers up the walls, as well as adding plants to the centre of the garden and among the cracks of paving.

Create habitats

Collections of pots offer lots of cool, damp hiding places between and underneath them for wildlife – put your pots on 'feet' if possible, as it helps drainage too. Supplementary homes such as bug and bee hotels, and bird and bat boxes, can be fixed to walls and fences. Incorporate water if possible, with a container pond or a bird bath.

Leaving an untidy corner is more difficult in a confined space where everything is on show, but a pile of leaves at the back of a bed or behind a corner of pots will go a long way toward helping wildlife. Where possible, connect your garden to your neighbour's and the wider world with access points in the bottom of fences.

Stagger the heights of your potted plants, with tall plants such as bamboo at the back

Wild garden paths and paving

Planting around paths and courtyards creates miniature corridors for your garden's smallest inhabitants; a sheltered (if convoluted) means of getting around without the risk of crossing a large, exposed slab of stone. No area is too small to be made wildlife friendly!

The easiest way to wild an area of garden paving is to stop weeding between the paving stones, but for something more uniform, floriferous and fragrant, the gaps can be deliberately planted instead. Either start with just the areas of loose mortar and let the plants spread themselves or, on flat areas of paving, where it's safer to disturb the integrity of the paving, deliberately chip out the mortar and plant everywhere. Once the mortar is removed, fill the cracks with a mixture of sand and soil or compost. Sow seeds into this or add in plants.

Selective planting

Another option is to lift up one or more paving slabs (in a pattern if you like) and put in planting instead. Lever out the stones carefully, and then dig out the sub-base, refilling the hole with a mixture of soil and compost. Plant as below or with herbs, drought-tolerant plants (see page 63) or a tree, or create a mini-wildflower meadow (pages 100–101) or pond (pages 116–117).

Alternatively, make a path using only plants such as those opposite. Stepping stones or stone car trackways can help to reduce wear on the plants, keep your shoes dry and avoid squashing wildlife.

Scatter seed

Low-growing plants for paths and paving

When planting into narrow cracks and gaps, divide the plant into several smaller pieces. Providing each has some root attached, it should grow. Washing the potting compost off the roots can help to fit them into a narrow planting space, and water well after planting to help bed them in. The simplest choice is grass, but to make it more interesting for insects and you, add some of these:

Clover

Thyme *Thymus*
For sunny areas: use the creeping types such as *Thymus serpyllum* or T. Coccineus Group.

Chamomile
Chamemelum nobile
The variety 'Trenague' is used for chamomile lawns, but it doesn't flower.

Clover *Trifolium*
Bees love the flowers, and you might find a lucky four-leafed clover!

Chamomile

Wild garden hero

Mexican fleabane (*Erigeron karvinskianus*) delights in self-seeding into paving cracks. It produces masses of tiny white and pink daisy-type flowers all summer and well into autumn, which are especially popular with hoverflies.

Ajuga

Creeping Jenny
Lysimachia nummularia 'Aurea'
Brings a golden brightness to shady areas.

Bugle *Ajuga reptans*
Grows well in shady areas, with dark blue flowers in summer.

Wild balconies and windowsills

Even the smallest window box can have some benefit for wildlife provided it contains suitable plants, and a balcony can be a relative oasis for insects and birds in a high-rise 'desert'. When growing above ground level, the first consideration is safety. Ensure the weight (when wet) of all your containers does not exceed your building's safe limits and that everything is securely fixed.

The second consideration is the exposure and wind levels that can cause plants to dry out quickly and/or their leaves to scorch. If possible, shelter balconies from the prevailing wind, either with a woven willow screen or some shrubby evergreen plants that can give shelter both to the other plants and to birds and bugs.

Wildlife up high

Wildlife that will visit a balcony is going to be creatures that can fly, and perhaps a very determined squirrel, so cater for insects and birds (see pages 70–71). A collection of plants in containers, including growing up walls and trailing over the balcony edge or railings, is a great start. Enrich the area with small log piles; insects will hide in them and birds perch on them. Add bird feeders and a bird bath or container pond where possible,

Use balcony railings for hanging additional planters and boxes, and for growing plants up and/or over.

Plants can spill
over window
boxes for
maximum effect

plus bug hotels and bird boxes on the walls
to tempt visitors into becoming residents.

Plants that have evolved to survive coastal
conditions are good choices for balconies,
such as rosemary (*Salvia rosmarinus*), and
anything with oily, waxy, narrow, small or
silvery leaves that minimises water loss,
such as lavender (*Lavandula*). Bulbs are a
great choice for spring, and will cope well
with shadier conditions.

Pollinator-friendly window boxes

A window box spilling over with flowering
plants can be buzzing with insect life from
spring to autumn, and will, perhaps, also
attract the odd avian visitor looking for

a meal. If possible, add hanging baskets on
brackets either side of your window and/or
a bird feeder or two to enhance your wild
windowsill garden further.

Although annuals (bedding) are the
traditional choice for window boxes,
and an easy way to ring the seasonal changes,
long-lasting flowering perennial plants are
a more sustainable and lower-maintenance
choice. Choose some upright plants and/or
some lower-growing or trailing ones to spill
over the edge, such as ivy (*Hedera helix*),
prostrate rosemary (*Salvia rosmarinus*
Prostratus Group), strawberries, fuchsias
(*Fuchsia*) or perennial sweet peas (*Lathyrus*).

Pot plants for pollinators

A single pot of seasonal flowers can bring not only pollinating insects and wildlife to your front or back door, but also some cheer to you as well. If you have space, invest in four or five planters so that you can wheel out the one that's looking best in each season and have the opportunity to refresh any annual and biennial plants in the others behind the scenes.

Crocus

Winter/early spring

Snowdrops
Galanthus nivalis
Can be flowering in January, ready for emerging bumblebees.

Snowdrops

Christmas rose
Helleborus or hybrids
Cut back the foliage in November to prevent the spread of diseases and make the flowers more prominent.

Hellebore

Crocus
Flowers only open when it's sunny and warm enough for bees to be active.

Daphne
Daphne odora
Scented flowers.

Daphne

Late spring

Aubretia
Aubrieta species
Plant around the pot edge for a cascading effect.

Aubretia

Foxgloves *Digitalis*
Bumblebees love the flowers of this biennial.

Foxgloves

Honesty *Lunaria annua*
White flowers will attract moths.

Honesty

Lungwort

Lungwort
Pulmonaria officinalis
Low-growing and shade-tolerant, this will carpet the base of a container and provide flowers for bees.

Early summer

Ornamental *Allium* cultivars
Big flower heads provide a lot of nectar in a small space.

Allium

Borage *Borago officinalis*
Stake if necessary; bees love the starry blue flowers.

Borage

Catmint *Nepeta*
Cut back after flowering for a second flush; 'Walker's Low' is a compact variety.

Catmint

Late summer

Japanese anemone
Anemone x hybrida cultivars
Flower from summer into autumn.

Japanese anemone

Vervain *Verbena bonariensis*
Slender plants; flowers visited by butterflies.

Verbena

Michaelmas daisy

Michaelmas daisy
Symphyotrichum novi-belgii
Masses of flowers; choose a single-flowered cultivar.

Autumn

Rudbeckia

Rudbeckia
Rudbeckia hirta, e.g.
'Toto' Herbaceous perennial that can be grown as an annual; flowers available in a range of autumnal tones.

Actaea *Actaea simplex*
Atropurpurea Group
Purple foliage sets off yellow rudbeckia flowers; tall spires of fragrant flowers are followed by berries.

Actaea

Wildlife-friendly edibles in containers

Food crops for ourselves – fruit, vegetables or herbs – can also provide a meal for pollinating insects (and, unfortunately, the odd slug or snail), as well as making attractive annual and perennial container displays.

If you've only room or the budget for small containers, it's best to stick to one or two crops per pot, but larger containers can be planted with a variety of species. It's also best not to mix perennials with annuals, to avoid disturbing the roots of the former when removing the latter at the end of the season.

What to grow

Many herbs are very happy growing in containers and, in the case of mint, which can spread easily, are sometimes better grown in pots.

Create a miniature forest garden by planting a cordon fruit tree (look for 'patio' or 'ballerina' varieties) in the centre of a large pot, and adding herbs and/or alpine strawberries around the base. Add more pots of underplanted fruit trees to build up a courtyard orchard full of spring blossom and autumn fruit.

Currants and soft fruit also offer plenty of flowers for pollinators early in the season – choose dwarf varieties of blackcurrants; white

and redcurrants and gooseberries can be trained/pruned into upright forms suitable for smaller pots. Plant breeders have also introduced new compact and bush forms of raspberry and blackberry plants suitable for growing in containers, and strawberries are ideal for pots and hanging baskets.

The legume family provides quality nectar and pollen for bees and other insects, so include these plants if possible, especially runner beans and broad beans, but also heritage/open-pollinated peas and dwarf or climbing French beans, mange tout or borlotti beans for drying. Climbing beans can be grown up a wigwam in a freestanding pot or up a trellis behind a rectangular planter along a wall or fence. Regular picking of climbing and runner beans encourages more flowers to form, keeping them in bloom until the first frosts.

The flowers of tomatoes and aubergines also attract insects, and give the best results for pollination. There are plenty of varieties suitable for pot growing, including dwarf tomatoes for windowsills and tumbling and/or trailing types that suit hanging baskets.

Water in a wild container garden

A container or courtyard garden can still offer water to wildlife – bird baths, bee drinkers and hoverfly lagoons (see pages 114–115) are self-contained and can be incorporated into a group of pots, or you can create a mini container pond.

Container pond

1 Container An ideal container will be watertight and large enough to include some aquatic plants – these will provide shelter and food for aquatic wildlife and help to keep the water clear.

2 Levels If possible, use something that has multiple levels/depths, but if not, create these using submerged bricks or stones: the shallows of a pond are the area favoured by most wildlife.

3 Base Add a layer of washed gravel at the base.

4 Entrances and exits It is crucial that any creature that gets in the pond is also able to get out. Containers often have steep, slippery sides, so build up stepping stones and or put in a ramp (use untreated wood) to help them escape easily.

5 Ramp or ladder A ramp or brick ladder up the outside of the pond will enable amphibians to get in the pond.

6 Pots Cluster other pots around the pond to encourage its use, ease access and provide shelter for creatures travelling to and from it.

7 Fountain A small fountain (solar-powered) can help keep the water clear and add interest, but isn't essential.

8 Topping up Fill and top up with rainwater, or leave tap water to stand in a bucket for at least 48 hours before adding to the pond.

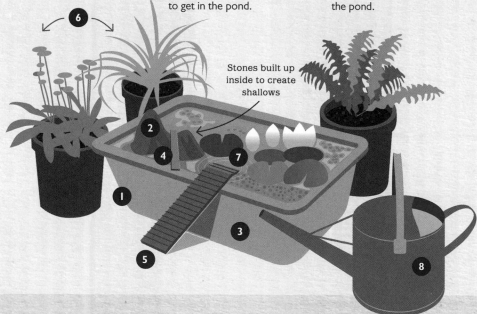

Stones built up inside to create shallows

Plants for a container pond

Use one oxygenating plant per square metre of pond surface, plus two marginals or a marginal and a water lily. A variety of leaf shapes and plant forms will allow for lots of different hiding places for wildlife, as well as visual aesthetic interest.

Oxygenators

Water violet

Water violet
Hottonia palustris

Hair grass
Eleocharis acicularis

Marginals

Dwarf rush
Juncus ensifolius

Sweet flag
Acorus gramineus var. pusillus

Sweet flag

Forget-me-not

Brooklime
Veronica beccabunga

Water forget-me-not
Myosotis scorpioides

Miniature water lilies

Nymphaea
'Pygmaea Helvola'
N. odorata var. minor

Water lilies

TREES, HEDGES AND EDGES
The benefits of trees

From bumblebees buzzing around spring blossom to beetles helping break down dead wood, a single tree can support many thousands of insects often in a diverse web of life several hundred species strong. The sheer volume of flowers on a tree is unrivalled for the space on the ground it takes up. Some trees have insects that rely on them particularly, such as the holly blue butterfly, which feed on holly trees as caterpillars. Insects and other minibeasts feed on trees' nectar and pollen, foliage, wood — and each other.

Birds are the most visible wildlife beneficiary of trees as they hop and flutter about their branches, safe from predators below. Birds use trees to nest and roost in, but also as sources of food — be that fruit, seeds, nuts or insects and bugs — nesting material and a place to perch and entertain us with their song.

Other wildlife also benefits from trees. Squirrels nest within boughs and feed on nuts the tree provides. Mice and badgers happily gorge on autumn fruits and nuts to lay on reserves for the cold winter ahead. Bats roost in hollow trunks, often sharing with woodpeckers. Finally, fungi and soil fauna feed on (decompose) the leaf litter and fallen branches, while mosses, lichens and parasitic plants such as mistletoe colonise the branches above, providing yet more varied habitats and food sources for the insects and birds.

Further uses

For us, trees bring wildlife, structure and
shade to a garden, and can also protect
us from noise and air pollution. Trees are
also beautiful. The seasons of a broadleaf
(deciduous) tree from stark winter branches,
through spring blossom, summer greens and
dappled sunshine, to autumn's fiery blaze is
one of nature's finest spectacles.

In addition, trees are one of nature's greatest
carbon-capture mechanisms, locking up
carbon not only in their trunks and branches,
but also in the leaves that fall and are
incorporated into the soil.

Trees for blossom, berry, seed and shelter

To make sure a tree is not going to outgrow its space, choose one with an appropriate ultimate height and spread. Some trees are naturally smaller, and fruit trees can be limited by choosing one with a dwarfing rootstock. Fruit trees can also be grown (trained) against walls and fences or even grown in large pots – there are options for even the smallest of spaces.

Some species, such as birch, grow faster than others. You may also want to consider if the tree is likely to seed widely into the garden – sycamores and ash are common culprits here. Trees that are commonly found in the area/country will be more likely to be used by the local wildlife than species from different climes. While evergreens offer more shelter and usually some kind of food for birds, broadleaved trees provide blossom in the spring and fruit or seeds/nuts in the autumn, so tend to offer more benefit for wildlife (though plant both, if you've space).

Apple blossom

Cherry/damson/plum
Birds and insects such as wasps enjoy the fruit; bees love the spring blossom.

Small to medium trees for blossom and fruit

Alder buckthorn
Frangula alnus
Blossom in spring, berries loved by thrushes in autumn; primary larval food plant of the brimstone butterfly.

Alder buckthorn

Apple
Blossom in spring can be staggered through different cultivars; birds like the fruit.

Ripe pears

Pear
Early spring blossom and good autumn colour.

Crab apple
Malus sylvestris cultivars
Blossom is followed by fruit enjoyed by birds such as robins, thrushes and finches.

Hawthorn
Crataegus laevigata or
C. monogyna
Berries hold well, providing winter food for birds such as fieldfares and redwings; caterpillars of many butterfly and moth species feed on the leaves.

Juneberry, or serviceberry

Juneberry
Amelanchier lamarckii
White blossom and stunning autumn foliage.

Sloe/Blackthorn
Prunus spinosa
Very early blossom provides vital nectar; autumn fruits eaten by birds, wasps and mammals; thorny branches protect nests and the foliage is a food plant for many moth caterpillars.

Cotoneaster

Cotoneaster
Cotoneaster 'Cornubia'
This particular cultivar can form a small tree if crown lifted; semi-evergreen and providing blossom and berries.

Wayfaring tree
Viburnum lantana
Umbelliferous spring blossom, then autumn berries loved by birds and small mammals but poisonous to humans.

Whitebeam *Sorbus aria*
Attractive blossom and scarlet berries in autumn; very popular with birds.

Whitebeam

Small to medium trees for seeds and nuts

Birch *Betula*
Provide a habitat for 500+ insect species, 100+ of which are exclusive to birch; these insects and the seeds attract birds; quick to grow but also senesce – dead wood is good for beetles and woodpeckers.

Hazel *Corylus avellana*
Leaves are food for caterpillars, the nuts food for mice (including the endangered hazel dormouse) and squirrels.

Wild garden hero

Rowan trees (*Sorbus aucuparia*) are an ideal choice for a small wild garden. They require little to no pruning and are attractive trees, with different cultivars offering different shades of berries. These berries are as popular with birds in the autumn as the blossom is with pollinators in the spring. They also host a variety of insect species that birds use to feed their growing chicks.

Walnut tree
Walnut tree

Large trees for blossom and fruit

Mulberries

Wild service tree
Sorbus torminalis
Relatively rare in the wild, with spring blossom then brown fruits that can be digested by birds but require bletting to be palatable to humans.

Mulberry *Morus rubra*
Tiny flowers; fruit soon drops to the ground, where it can be eaten by small mammals.

Wild cherry *Prunus avium*
Plentiful blossom and fruit for birds.

Large trees for blossom, seeds and nuts

Linden flowers

Linden/lime
Tilia cordata or *T.* x *europaea*
Fragrant flowers loved by bees; foliage loved by aphids – use the tree to attract aphid predators such as hoverflies and ladybirds.

Beech *Fagus sylvatica*
The nuts/seeds ('masts') provide autumn food for mammals and birds such as nuthatch and chaffinch.

Walnut *Juglans*
Autumn nuts loved by squirrels and mice; leaves are a caterpillar food plant for many species of moth.

Sweet chestnut
Castanea sativa
Mice and squirrels eat the nuts; various micro-moth species feed on the leaves and nuts.

Horse chestnuts

Horse chestnut
Aesculus hippocastanum
Flowers rich in nectar; conkers eaten by mammals; leaves eaten by various caterpillars, which in turn are favoured by blue tits.

Bird cherry blossom

Bird cherry *Prunus padus*
Blossom followed by fruit loved by blackbirds, song thrushes, badgers and mice.

Alder *Alnus glutinosa*
Flowers provide early pollen for bees; seeds are enjoyed by siskin, finches and red poll.

Acorns on oak tree

Spruce *Picea*
Home to a variety of invertebrates and caterpillars of moth species; these in turn provide food for goldcrests; seeds eaten by red squirrels.

Holly *Ilex*
Provides berries and winter shelter for birds; leaves are food for caterpillars, including the holly blue.

Holly berries

Oak *Quercus*
Long-lived trees providing plenty of standing dead wood for invertebrates; acorns are winter food for squirrels and mice.

Evergreen trees for food and shelter

Yew *Taxus baccata*
Dense foliage and red berries (toxic to humans) for birds in autumn.

Pine *Pinus*
Tall trees provide shelter for birds; pine resin is used by bees to make propolis for their hives.

Pine cones and needles

Growing trees large and small

Having chosen a tree or trees for your garden, investing time into planting them well will ensure their success for many years to come.

Buying trees

Young trees (one or two years old) establish and grow quickly, require less watering and aftercare, and are more resilient than older potted specimens, so, after five years there would be little to tell between them.

Young trees like this can be bought relatively inexpensively, especially if they are bought 'bare root' (i.e. not potted in compost)

during the winter dormant season. Choose healthy-looking trees with well-developed roots; if it is potted take it out of the pot to check it's not rootbound. Avoid anything with dead branches or tips.

Planting

Ideally, plant in autumn or early winter, when the soil is still warm and the rain will keep it moist. This gives the tree time to root into the soil before spring. Soak bare-root plants in a bucket of water for a few hours before planting.

Soak the roots
before planting

Dig the hole not too deep, and wide enough to accommodate all the roots without bending them – trees like to have their roots running outward just under the surface. Work a garden fork into the soil at the base and sides of the hole if it is very compacted (e.g. in the middle of a lawn), but otherwise try not to disturb it too much. Mix a little compost with the soil and back-fill around the roots, heeling it in firmly. Water it well and mulch around the base with a little more compost (make sure it doesn't touch the trunk).

Stake young trees with a hazel stake or cane – tie it on loosely in a couple of places to allow the tree to rock a little in the wind. This will help it to grow a strong base so the support can be removed in a couple of years' time. Larger specimens will need a stronger stake and a cushioned tie.

Aftercare

Water newly planted trees during dry spells, and mulch annually. Check ties and loosen or replace them twice-yearly. Most trees (except fruit trees) won't need much pruning except to remove diseased wood. It is usually advised to also remove dead wood, but if it is safe and you are happy with the look, you may choose to leave it as a valuable habitat.

The benefits of hedges

Hedges are by far the best wildlife-friendly boundary, offering food, shelter and nesting sites to a wide range of creatures. In a garden design, hedges can also divide a space into garden rooms, give structure to larger spaces and make small gardens appear bigger.

moths lay their eggs on larval food plants. Some insects are specific to hedge species, such as the brown hairstreak butterfly, whose caterpillars eat only blackthorn leaves. These insects are food for other insects and for birds, some of which will also eat the berries, seeds and nuts. The dense, often spiky branches provide nesting sites for birds, too, protected from predators.

Along the base of a hedge will scurry mice and voles, hedgehogs and amphibians, which use the shelter it provides as a corridor from place to place, and the gaps allow them to move to and from your garden to other

Hedges are a superb carbon sink, absorbing up to c1.2 tonnes (1.3 tons) of carbon each year (for 100m/328ft of mature mixed hedge), while slowing winds and rain run-off.

Hedges are great at absorbing noise and/or air pollution too – let them get 1.5m (5ft) high and 1m (3ft) thick at least, and/or plant a double hedge to help in this regard.

A hedge is a whole ecosystem within itself; it provides so many benefits for wildlife. Numerous insects and invertebrates will make their homes within it. Pollinating insects feed on the flowers, and butterflies and

Hedges provide safe cover

gardens and the wider landscape. Above, in the night sky, bats use hedges (and other linear features) to help them navigate.

Smaller hedges are a great way to edge or divide areas of the garden and provide sheltered corridors for wildlife. Flowering shrubs such as lavender (*Lavandula*), rosemary (*Salvia rosmarinus*), hedge germander (*Teucrium* x *lucidys*) and Christmas box (*Sarcococca confusa*) are all good choices.

Underplanting a hedge with perennials and spring bulbs adds more flowers to the space for you and wildlife. Try primroses (*Primula vulgaris*), snowdrops (*Galanthus nivalis*) and lungwort (*Pulmonaria officinalis*).

Cutting and laying hedges

Hedges should only be cut outside the nesting season – that is, between early autumn and late winter. Check along the hedge just to be sure before cutting if possible – with seasonal weather changes, it's possible some birds will have a late brood. Ideally, cut a mixed deciduous hedge every other year to allow plenty of flowers and berries to develop, or better still, lay it instead.

Laying is a traditional agricultural technique that looks brutal but actually helps to regenerate the hedge, and keep it healthy and full. Different regions have their own styles, some of which include inserting upright stakes and weaving a top section to hold them steady. There are online tutorials showing how to do it – the usual tool is a billhook – or seek advice from hedge laying associations and local craftspeople.

Plants for a wild-garden hedge

Any hedge is better for wildlife than a bare wall or fence, and the plants below all make good hedges, either planted as a single species or mixed together. A hedge of mixed deciduous species is considered the best for wildlife in that it can offer varied food as well as nesting places, but evergreens such as yew can also bear berries and give year-round shelter. Beech and hornbeam hedges are deciduous, but keep their old leaves on through winter. The choice depends on the space available and the design of your garden. If planting a mixed hedge, aim for two-thirds of one species (usually supplied as hawthorn in pre-mixed batches) and the rest another five or more species.

KEY

❀ deciduous
🌿 evergreen
♧ semi-evergreen
✿ flowers
🍒 fruit/berries
◐ nuts/seeds
☁ especially good at absorbing pollution

Sloes, the fruit of blackthorn

Maple leaf

Elder *Sambucus nigra*
❀ ✿ 🍒

Field maple
Acer campestre
❀ ✿ ◐

Fruit trees and bushes, e.g. currants, wild pears, crab apple and cherry
❀ ✿ 🍒

Guelder rose
Viburnum opulus
❀ ✿ 🍒

Viburnum

Autumnal beech

Blackthorn
Prunus spinosa
❀ ✿ 🍒

Cotoneaster
☁ ✿ 🍒

Dogwood
Cornus sanguinea
❀

Beech
Fagus sylvatica
❀

Dogwood

Hawthorn
Crataegus monogyna,
C. laevigata
❀ ✿ 🍒

Common hazel

Hazel *Corylus avellana*
❀ ✿ ◗

Hedgehog rose *Rosa rugosa*
❀/🍃 ✿ 🍒

Holly *Ilex aquifolium*
🍃 ✿ 🍒

Hornbeam *Carpinus betulus*
❀

Springtime hornbeam

Privet, Wild privet
Ligustrum ovalifolium,
L. vulgare
❀/🍃 ✿ 🍒 🌰

Sea buckthorn
Hippophae rhamnoides
❀ ✿ 🍒

Bullace
Prunus insititia
❀ ✿ 🍒

Spindle
Euonymus europaeus
❀ ✿ 🍒

Spindle berries

Western red cedar
Thuja plicata
🍃 🌰

Western cedar

Viburnum
Viburnum bodnantense,
V. tinus, V. opulus
❀/🍃 ✿ 🍒

Yew *Taxus baccata*
🍃 🍒 🌰

Climbing/ scrambling plants to grow through a hedge

Blackberry *Rubus fruticosus*
❀ ✿ 🍒

Dog rose hips

Dog rose *Rosa canina*
❀ ✿ 🍒

Honeysuckle
Lonicera periclymenum
❀/E 🍃 ✿

Ivy *Hedera helix*
🍃 ✿ 🍒

Old man's beard
Clematis vitalba or
C. tangutica 'Bill Mackenzie'
❀/🍃 ✿ N

Winter clematis
C. 'Jingle Bells', *C.* 'Winter Beauty'
❀/🍃 ✿ ◗

Winter clematis

Vertical growing: climbing plants and green walls

A bare wall or fence can still provide places to nest and perch. Mason bees and plasterer bees, as their names suggest, will nest in holes or crumbling mortar, and walls can house bird and bat boxes. However, adding plants offers more food, shelter and nesting sites for a much wider range of wildlife.

There are two types of plants that can be grown up a wall or fence: those that will cling on themselves, using sucker pads and roots, and those that need supporting and tying in (put wires etc. on the wall before planting). Many climbers can be used to provide autumn and winter flowers, and evergreen species will offer more shelter, but when selecting a plant, take into account how much sun it will need and its vigour.

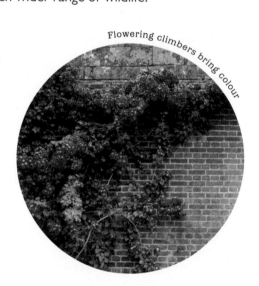

Flowering climbers bring colour

Greening garden walls

Other options for greening a wall include adding structures in which perennials and annuals can be grown, such as old pallets or guttering, shelves, hanging baskets or fabric pockets used to create blocks of plants.

These bring big benefits to the environment and the home, as well as wildlife.

Tiny plants (ferns and succulents) can be planted into the cracks in stone walls. Shallow-rooted species will do little damage, such as *Alyssum*, *Asplenium trichomanes*, *Asplenium ruta-muraria* and *Echeveria*. Moss will grow over any shady, damp wall; by blitzing moss and yoghurt in a blender then painting it on the wall, you can speed up colonisation (search online for 'moss graffiti').

Natural climbers

Plants that don't need support

Virginia creeper
and Boston ivy
Parthenocissus species

Climbing hydrangeas
Hydrangea anomola subsp.
petiolaris and *Pileostegia*
vibrunoides

Trumpet vine

Trumpet vine
Campsis radicans

Plants that need support

Roses *Rosa*

Jasmine
Jasminum and
Trachelospermum

Jasmine

Wild garden hero

Common ivy (*Hedera helix*) is
a superb plant to have in a wild
garden – and will grow in almost
any situation. Its dense evergreen
foliage traps air pollution and
provides year-round cover for
insects, invertebrates and birds.
Its autumn flowers and subsequent
berries provide late-season food for
many creatures. When grown on a
house wall, research shows it keeps
homes cooler in summer and less
damp in winter.

Firethorn *Pyracantha*

Passionflower *Passiflora*

Passionflower

Wisteria

Honeysuckle
Lonicera pericylmenum

Summer clematis

Summer-flowering clematis
Autumn and winter-
flowering clematis
e.g. *Clematis tangutica* 'Bill
Mackenzie', *C. cirrhosa*

Wall-trained fruit trees

Honeysuckle

Wilder garden buildings

Garden buildings large or small can all be made greener, which not only makes them more attractive to wildlife but also to us, helping to blend them in to the wider garden landscape or just look prettier. Bin stores, bike and garden sheds, summerhouses, home offices and end-of-the-garden entertaining and gym spaces can all have climbers grown up their walls and nesting boxes for birds and bees added to them (see pages 126–130). Just make sure that boxes are out of reach of potential predators, such as cats on the roof.

Pre-grown rolls and tiles of green-roof matting can be purchased for an easy option – *Sedum* species are often used, but the more variety of flowers the roof offers, the greater its appeal.

Adding a green roof to a garden building

It's possible to add plants to a roof surface, especially with small structures such as bin stores. Green roofs can weigh over 100kg (220lb) per square metre, and anything larger than a small shed should have the approval of a structural engineer to ensure that the building will safely withstand the weight of the roof. Ideally the roof would be gently sloping, to aid drainage.

Cover the roof with a heavy-duty waterproofing material such as butyl pond liner. Leave some overhang to go up the sides of the frame once it's been built. Build a timber box frame to go around the area to be covered, securely screwed to the roof. Most herbs will grow well in a depth of around 15–18cm (6–8in), but sedums will cope in a 10cm- (4in-) deep frame. Drill drainage holes at regular intervals in the frame.

Fill the frame with a layer of gravel, crushed shells or other drainage material (avoid perlite, which has a high carbon footprint), topped with a layer of peat-free compost. Plant with herbs such as thyme (*Thymus*), wildflower perennials and grasses (see page 98) or succulents.

Tiny succulents thrive with little water or soil

Greenhouses

The one garden building that can't be made wildlife-friendly on the outside is a greenhouse. However, encouraging insects inside helps with pollination of crops and provides early-season nectar for them — advertise its presence using bright flowers such as marigolds (*Calendula, Tagetes*). Providing shelter for toads and frogs will mean some resident slug control as well.

LAWNS

Sustainable and wildlife-friendly lawns

Natural grassland is an important carbon sink, locking away atmospheric carbon almost as effectively as trees. A lawn is more wildlife-friendly than paving, decking or Astroturf, and with a few simple tweaks you can create a beautiful lawn-based habitat.

The first step toward making a lawn more sustainable and wildlife-friendly is to embrace its diversity. There is a traditional preoccupation with lawns that prioritises the monoculture of grass over supposed 'weed' (i.e. flower) species and moss. However, it is impossible to eliminate the flowers completely or forever, and it is much better for insects and other species if we stop using chemical herbicides and fertilisers to try and achieve it. You'll also save time, effort and money.

Wild lawn options

To turn an existing lawn a bit wilder, the simplest choice is to stop mowing it, or to cut only some areas once a month or even once a year (see pages 102–103). A variety of heights is best, so it's still possible to maintain an area of short grass for children to play on or for entertaining. Reducing the vigour of the grass will help flower species. To enhance an existing lawn with more flowers, add perennial flowers as seed, young plug plants and/or bulbs (see pages 97–99).

To create a new lawn and/or meadow area on bare soil in a sunny spot, sowing annual cornfield flowers will give the most instant results but they might not perform well in the following years and need additional seed (see

Vary grass height

page 96). Perennial flowers and grasses from seed (see page 98) or plug plants (page 94) creates a low-maintenance meadow over time but is likely to look a bit bare to begin with.

Wildlife in a lawn

The flowers in a meadow provide food for bees, butterflies and other insects. Butterflies and moths will lay their eggs on larval food plants such as clover. Ground beetles and solitary bees will live in the tussocky bases of the grasses, and grasshoppers sing from the stems. The predators of these species, and the worms and grubs (such as chafer grubs) beneath the soil, attract birds, frogs and hedgehogs, while mice and voles eat the seeds and use the grass and moss for their nests.

Adding wildflowers to a lawn

It can be trickier to add wildflowers into an existing lawn than to start afresh with bare ground, but it's not impossible. A perennial meadow is the best option, as it will grow stronger every year, and there may already be flowers in the lawn that will thrive too, such as daisies and buttercups.

Lawn preparation

The best time for establishing a meadow is autumn. During the preceding spring and summer, mow using the lawnmower's lowest setting, collect the clippings and rake the grass thoroughly, regularly. Grasses are an important part of the meadow but can easily outcompete the flowers, so reducing their vigour and the soil fertility they like is key to the success of a meadow.

Planting plugs

An easy option is to sow seed over the top of the grass in autumn (see page 96). Alternatively, you can set out trays ('plugs') or small pots – either grown by a plant nursery or by yourself from seed. These flower species will already have had a chance to grow to a decent size before they have to compete with the grass and are likely to get off to a better start to flower the following year. Bulbs could also be added and overseed with yellow rattle to weaken the grass further. (See pages 97–99 for profiles of wildflowers suited to lawns.)

Plant the plugs in early autumn, into ground prepared as above. Use five plants per square metre, in drifts or groups of the same species for a more natural look. Remove a small divot using a trowel or bulb planter, and place in the plant. Backfill with a low-nutrient or seed compost, firm in well and water. It may be necessary to hand-weed out the grasses around them for the first season to allow them space to establish.

Cowslip plugs

Wild garden hero

Yellow rattle (*Rhinanthus minor*) is a pretty annual wildflower that taps into the roots of neighbouring grasses, thereby reducing the availability of water and nutrients to them as it grows; it has been called a 'floral vampire'. Having yellow rattle in a meadow can suppress the grass by as much as 60 per cent, allowing other species to flourish in their stead. It must be sown in later summer and early autumn from fresh seed or it won't germinate. Allow it to set seed before mowing in the autumn and leave the clippings for a week to let the seed fall to the ground before raking off the cuttings. Other, less effective grass parasite species include *Euphrasia* (eyebright) and lousewort (*Pedicularis paulustris* and *P. sylvatica*).

Buy fresh
You must buy this seed fresh or it won't germinate – use a grower you can trust.

Wildflower meadows from seed and turf

Scattering seed or rolling out an established mat of meadow plants is a lot easier than planting plug plants, and both are a good option for establishing a new area of meadow from scratch.

Sowing a wildflower meadow

Start work on a perennial meadow in autumn or spring, or in spring for an annual meadow. If the area is currently grassed, strip off the turf by hand or with a purpose-built machine. Stack the turf strips grass-side down to make a mound with no visible green grass – they will rot down into a pile of topsoil. Rake the soil and leave it bare for six weeks, then weed thoroughly. Rake smooth again and water. Bare soil need only be weeded, raked and watered. Check the packet for the correct density of seed per square metre. Scatter the seed thinly over the area. Rake over gently to ensure good contact between seeds and soil.

Using meadow turf

Square-metre strips of pre-grown meadow plants are sold like grass turf (by online suppliers) and come in various mixes. Prepare the soil as above so you can lay the turf the day it arrives. Cover the central area first, then cut in the edges with smaller sections, butting up the edges firmly to knit the sections together. Water well initially and regularly until the turf has rooted into the soil.

Mix seed with sand so it's easier to see where you've already sown.

Wildflowers: annuals and bulbs

True wildflower meadows are made up of grasses and perennials, but the colourful annual wildflower seed mixes (usually cornfield flowers, arable weeds) can give a burst of summer colour that is popular with pollinating insects. Most bulbs will grow in grass, but these are the ones particularly suited to it.

Annuals

California poppy
Eschscholzia californica

California poppy

Cornflower
Centaurea cyanus

Field poppy
Papaver rhoeas

Scorpion weed
Phacelia tanacetifolia

Scorpion weed

Corn marigolds

Corn marigold
Chrysanthemum segetum

Bulbs

Grocus

Crocus
Crocus tommasinianus for spring flowers; *C. pulchellus* for autumn

Snowdrops
Galanthus nivalis

Daffodil
Narcissus pseudonarcissus and *N.* 'Actaea'

Snake's head fritillary
Fritillaria meleagris

Fritillary

Tulips
Tulipa sprengeri and *T. sylvestris*

Camassia
Camassia leichtlinii subsp. *suksdorfii* Caerulea group

Wildflowers: perennials

Perennials (plants that come back year after year) are the plants that make up most of the meadow wildflower species and attract a wide range of insects to feed and live among their flowers and grasses, from butterflies to beetles, and hoverflies to grasshoppers. Here are some of the best perennial species to grow for a flower-rich meadow from spring to late summer; all will grow well on most·soil types. For meadow bulbs and annual flowers, see page 97.

Lawn preparation

The best time for establishing a meadow is autumn. During the preceding spring and summer mow using the lawnmower's lowest setting, collect the clippings and rake the grass thoroughly, regularly. Grasses are an important part of the meadow but can easily outcompete the flowers, so reducing their vigour and the soil fertility they like is key to the success of a meadow.

Red campion and ox-eye daisy

Cowslip

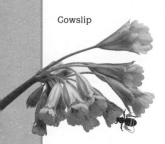

Cowslip
Primula veris
Pale yellow flowers
in spring.

Meadow buttercup
Ranunculus acris
Yellow flowers in late
spring and summer.

Red campion
Silene dioica
Pink flowers in
late spring.

Ox-eye daisy
Leucanthemum vulgare
Large white daisy flowers
in late spring/early summer.

Selfheal
Prunella vulgaris
Purple flowers from spring
to summer, best for areas
of short grass.

Bird's foot trefoil

Ground ivy
Glechoma hederacea
Blue/purple flowers in late
spring and summer; best for
areas of short grass.

Bird's foot trefoil
Lotus corniculatus
Yellow flowers from late
spring to early autumn;
best for short grass.

Glover

Clover

Trifolium pratense (purple/
red) and *T. repens* (white)
Flower all summer.

Field scabious

Knautia arvensis
Pale purple flowers in
summer to autumn.

Sorrel

Rumex acetosa
Edible leaves and flowers
in summer.

Knapweed

Centaurea nigra
Purple flowers in
summer.

Yarrow

Lady's bedstraw

Lady's bedstraw

Galium verum
Yellow flowers in late
summer on aromatic
foliage.

Betony

Betonica officinalis
Spikes of red/purple flowers
in late summer.

Hawkbits

Leontodon species
Yellow flowers in summer
and early autumn.

Field scabious

Yarrow and sneezewort

Achillea millefolium
and *A. ptarmica*
White umbel flowers
in summer, edible
leaves.

Meadow clary

Salvia pratensis
Spikes of pale purple
flowers in summer.

Hawkbits

Ground ivy

Meadow clary

Small-scale meadows and lawns

Wildflower meadows and flowering lawns as detailed earlier in this chapter do not need to be large or to take up the whole of the lawn space. In fact, patches of shorter, mown areas or paths among taller meadows can be an effective design and also allow birds to swoop in and feed on insects and worms in the shorter grass. It's also possible to create mini-meadows for a courtyard, balcony or other paved area, to bring a wilder beauty to the space and to attract pollinators and other insects.

Wildflower meadows in pots and growbags

Both annual and perennial mini-meadows can be created in a pot or – for a larger surface area – a growbag. Pots should have adequate drainage, and be at least 20cm (8in) deep, but the wider the top the better. Cut out most of the top of the growbag, leaving a frame of the bag to prevent the compost within being washed away, or fill a re-usable growbag with compost. A multi-purpose or seed compost is best.

Annual wildflower seed mixes are readily available, and in order that each plant has sufficient space to grow well, should be sown thinly over the top of the pot. Check the seed packet for the recommended sowing density for the area (grams per square metre), which is likely to be 1–5g per square metre, depending on the mix. Scatter the seed thinly over the top of pre-watered compost – mixing seeds with a little sand (more visible than the seed) can help to ensure an even coverage. Gently rake or press the surface to ensure good contact between compost and seeds.

Perennial meadows can be sown from seed as above, or young plants can be planted into containers, allowing around 6–8 plants per square metre.

Adding a lawn element to a patio

Meadow turf can be added into a patio by taking out some of the paving (in rented properties be sure to have permission or be able to replace it as it was). This can bring life to an otherwise barren desert of concrete and stone for insects, and there's the chance to create patterns of stone and meadow across the area. Before ordering, calculate which slabs to lift and the area in metres squared you will need of turf. Having carefully lifted and removed the paving slabs, dig out some of the stone if necessary and add a 10–20cm- (4–8in-) deep bed of low-nutrient compost or topsoil. Cut sections of perennial wildflower turf to fit and firm it in well, watering thoroughly afterwards.

Mowing and maintenance

Wild lawns cut to a range of different heights and with different mowing frequencies are the best option for wildlife because they encourage flowering as well as creating a variety of habitats and feeding opportunities. For example, butterflies appreciate areas of long grass and flowers, but blackbirds like short grass, where they can more easily pull up worms. In a small space, varying heights of grass can look messy, so leave some meadow long and cut the rest either monthly or weekly, or leave it all at the same height. Keep the soil fertility low by always collecting the clippings.

Larger perennial meadows/wild lawns mowing schedule

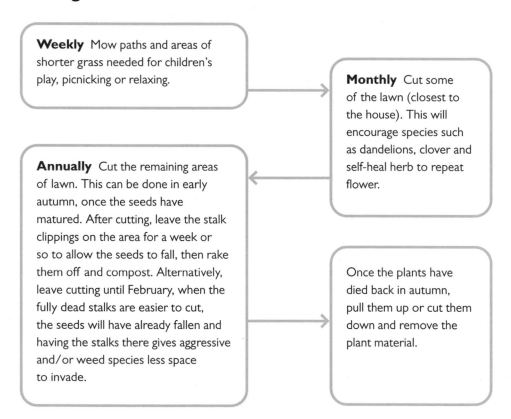

Weekly Mow paths and areas of shorter grass needed for children's play, picnicking or relaxing.

Monthly Cut some of the lawn (closest to the house). This will encourage species such as dandelions, clover and self-heal herb to repeat flower.

Annually Cut the remaining areas of lawn. This can be done in early autumn, once the seeds have matured. After cutting, leave the stalk clippings on the area for a week or so to allow the seeds to fall, then rake them off and compost. Alternatively, leave cutting until February, when the fully dead stalks are easier to cut, the seeds will have already fallen and having the stalks there gives aggressive and/or weed species less space to invade.

Once the plants have died back in autumn, pull them up or cut them down and remove the plant material.

Varying grass
height will suit
a wider variety
of wildlife and
their needs

Dock

Thistle

Other maintenance

Some species, such as docks, thistles and
nettles, are valuable plants for wildlife but
can be aggressive and take over a patch.
Keep a few, but deadhead them before
they seed and pull them up where they
have spread to keep them under control.

Fill in any gaps, especially in the early years,
with a little seed or more plug plants.

Nettle

EDIBLE GARDENS
A sustainable veg patch

Growing your own food is hugely rewarding, no matter the size of your veg patch. Homegrown organic veg can be harvested fresh for the best taste and nutritional values, and it reduces food miles and your carbon footprint. Encouraging a wilder kitchen garden means more pollinators for your crops, and predators for the pests.

Do you dig it?

Traditionally, veg plots were subjected to double-digging, which was mechanised by the rotavator. Today it is realised that by disturbing the soil so violently, the delicate ecosystems within it are ruptured, harming the health of the soil and releasing carbon into the atmosphere. Inevitably some of the soil fauna – worms, beetles and even sheltering frogs and toads – can get hurt as well. By following no-dig principles – essentially adding an annual layer of compost on top of the soil that worms turn in gradually – the soil can be improved naturally. Anecdotal evidence suggests no-dig beds produce heavier yields and have a better-quality topsoil.

Green manures

Another way to improve the soil naturally is to sow green manures on any patches that aren't being used over winter, which prevents nutrient loss through soil erosion. Green manures can also add nutrients – those in the bean family will fix nitrogen in the soil, such as clovers (*Trifolium* species) or winter tares (*Vicia sativa*). Clover and fiddleneck (*Phacelia tanacetifolia*) are extremely valuable to bees and other insects.

Green manures are usually cut down in spring and dug into the soil, but if you'd rather not dig, cut them off at the base and compost the top growth.

Productive, pest-free and perennial veg

To make the most of your space, grow efficient crops. Root crops sown direct into the soil (e.g. carrots and beetroot) are low maintenance and inexpensive to grow. Repeat or long-season plants such as courgettes and climbing beans give multiple crops over a long period. Perennial vegetables are those that can be harvested in a small way but over many years, such as salsify, Daubenton's kale, Babington's leek, Caucasian spinach (*Hablitzia tamnoides*) and crummock. They especially suit forest garden settings (see page 109). Some crops are also naturally less prone to pests, including pumpkins/squash, courgettes, beans, chard, rhubarb and blackcurrants.

Saving seeds

Growing heirloom and open-pollinated varieties and saving their seeds to plant the following year helps to ensure a legacy of diverse vegetable varieties, saves money and is quite empowering for the domestic grower to boot. Beans, peas, tomatoes and pumpkin/squash are easy ones to start with, and allowing a little of other crops to flower and seed, such as radishes, salads and leafy veg, is a good next step.

Winning plant combinations

When plants are grown together for a specific benefit, it is known as companion planting. This could be to deter or reduce the incidence of pests on a crop, to increase diversity in the garden both above and below ground, or to simply save space.

Many plants are thought to be good companions because of their ability to attract pollinating insects, pest predators (such as hoverflies and lacewing flies) or both. Others can deter pests through their strong-scented foliage. They can be good choices for a wild edible garden that doesn't use pesticides; experiment to find companions that work for you.

Some good companion plants are edible in themselves, others can be planted in a border around edibles, or under tall, thin plants such as tomatoes, sweetcorn or soft fruit bushes and canes.

Summer savory

Useful edible companion plants

Nasturtiums

Nasturtiums
Tropaeolum majus
Sacrificial plant for attracting whitefly and aphids; flowers attract pollinators.

Pot marigolds
Calendula officinalis
Flowers attract pollinators and pest predators.

Summer savory
Satureja hortensis
Foliage fragrance can deter aphids; flowers attract pollinators.

Garlic chives
Allium tuberosum
Foliage fragrance can deter pests; flowers attract pollinators; use the leaves to make a plant tea to protect against downy mildew.

Useful inedible companion plants

Marigolds
Tagetes patula, T. minuta
Foliage fragrance can deter aphids and whitefly; flowers attract pest predators; roots exude compounds toxic to perennial weeds.

Tobacco plant
Nicotiana tabacum
Foliage fragrance can deter cabbage white butterflies when inter-planted with brassicas.

Basil *Ocimum basilicum*
Foliage fragrance deters pests; use as a sacrificial plant for whitefly infestations; when interplanted it promotes the growth and flavour of aubergines, lettuce and tomatoes.

Borage *Borago officinalis*
Flowers attract pollinators and pest predators; promotes growth of strawberries; deters tomato hornworm. Edible flowers only.

Flowering basil

Mint
Mentha species
Foliage fragrance deters aphids, flea beetles, ants and other pests.

Tobacco plant

Herbs to attract bees and butterflies

Herbs are useful plants, for their culinary, medicinal, dyeing or scented properties. They also have an intrinsic appeal to wildlife, especially bees and butterflies but also many other insects including beetles and hoverflies. If you don't have space for a herb garden, many herbs suit container growing, or they can be incorporated in borders.

Flowering fennel

Fennel *Foeniculum vulgare*
Tall stems with yellow umbellifer flowers in late summer; hollow stems useful for overwintering insects when cut and left.

Mint *Mentha*
Cutting back the foliage in early summer to preserve for the kitchen results in later flowering, for useful end-of-season nectar.

Rosemary
Salvia rosmarinus or *Rosmarinus officinalis*
Flowers in late winter/early spring, especially useful for emerging bumblebees.

Oregano/marjoram
Origanum vulgare;
O. majorana
Sprawling plants popular with butterflies.

Lavender

Lemon balm
Melissa officinalis
Also known as bee balm, so popular is this plant with insects.

Teucrium

Lavender
Lavandula angustifolia
All cultivars of this species are loved by bees.

Comfrey
Symphytum officinale
Bumblebees especially like the flowers, and the leaves can be used to make a plant fertiliser (see page 41).

Sage *Salvia officinalis*
The flowers provide nectar over a long period in mid to late summer.

Thyme *Thymus vulgaris*
Small plants produce a mass of flowers. Creeping thyme can be grown in cracks of paving.

Teucrium *Teucrium species*
Inedible but scented, all species are popular with bees and other insects, often with long flowering periods.

Edible forest gardens

Edible forest gardening is a wildlife-friendly method of growing food –
especially fruit, nuts and herbs. Layers of planting – canopy trees, mid-level
shrubs and climbers, and lower-growing perennials mimicking a young, open
woodland – are used to offer diverse harvests over many years. Start from
scratch or retrofit additional layers around existing trees or shrubs.

Forest gardening works in harmony with nature and as such
is often used by permaculture gardeners, who design their
gardens to increase biodiversity and reduce humankind's
impact on the planet. Once planted, an edible forest garden
needs minimal maintenance, allowing it to become as wild
as possible.

The aim with a
forest garden is to leave
it relatively undisturbed
so the soil and wildlife
thrive.

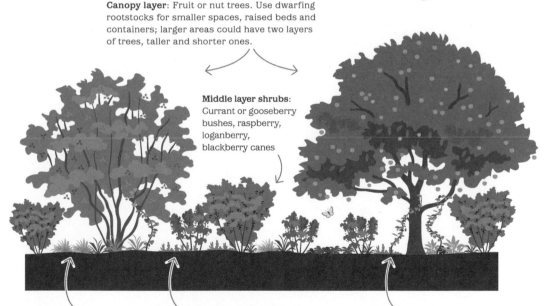

Canopy layer: Fruit or nut trees. Use dwarfing
rootstocks for smaller spaces, raised beds and
containers; larger areas could have two layers
of trees, taller and shorter ones.

Middle layer shrubs:
Currant or gooseberry
bushes, raspberry,
loganberry,
blackberry canes

Ground cover:
Violas, wild
strawberries,
wild garlic

Perennials: Herbs (mint, lemon
balm, chives), leafy and/or
perennial veg (chard, Daubenton's
kale), comfrey

Climbers: Such as kiwi fruit
or magnolia vine (*Schisandra
chinensis*) can also be
incorporated

Other ways to grow food

No matter the size of your plot, growing food in rows or large blocks of the same crop is essentially creating a patchwork supermarket for wildlife that would like to eat your harvests as much as you do. If instead you grow a little food here and a little there, disguising it among ornamentals, companion plants or just mixing up the crops, it can create an attractive jumble and result in far fewer losses to pests and diseases without the need for ugly mesh and other preventative measures.

Mixing up a veg patch

A polyculture veg patch is still a carefully ordered space. First, use both the vertical and horizontal planes, growing smaller plants such as beetroot, carrots or salad leaves or sprawling pumpkins and squash under tall thin crops such as sweetcorn, tomatoes and climbing beans.

Dividing a veg bed into smaller squares (such as in the 'square foot' gardening technique) and creating a patchwork potager of different crops will confuse pests. Growing edible or companion flowers among the crops and growing strongly scented plants in different places can also attract pollinators and predators while deterring pests (for example, the scent of shallots and garlic is thought to ward off carrot root fly).

Mixing into the borders

If your flower borders have space in them for annual plants, why not use the borders for edible crops? A small group of lettuces here, a wigwam of climbing beans there; many veg are attractive enough to be part of an ornamental display — just make sure they are easy to reach for picking.

Fruit trees and bushes are even easier to incorporate into a border and provide pretty blossom in the spring as well as autumn colour — step-over apples can be used along the front of a bed, or train fruit trees against a wall or fence at the back of a border.

Ornamental edibles and edible ornamentals

Food for looks and taste

Food that looks good

Beetroot 'Bull's Blood'
Attractive leaves make a good potager edging plant.

Rainbow chard
Colourful stems and leaf midribs.

Sea kale
Large glaucous leaves with crinkled edges.

Red cabbage
Deep colouring, leaves look wonderful when frosted.

Climbing French/runner beans
Pods and flowers in white or purple as well as green, or scarlet runner bean flowers.

Red/white/blackcurrants
Inconspicuous flowers followed by jewel-like fruits.

Blueberries
Grey-green foliage turns a brilliant red in autumn.

Rainbow chard

Red cabbage

Fruit trees
Pretty blossom and autumn colour as well as the fruit.

Herbs
Fragrant and floriferous, there are hundreds of herbs from which to choose.

Ornamentals that taste good

Buffalo currant
Ribes odoratum
A larger version of
a blackcurrant.

Elderflower
Sambucus
Edible flowers and fruit
(once cooked).

Autumn olive
Eleagnus umbellata
Juicy fruits follow spice-
scented flowers.

Buffalo currant

Cornelian cherry

Autumn olive

Cornelian cherry
Cornus mas
Low-maintenance spreading
shrub with cherry-like fruit.

Daylily
Hemerocallis fulva
Flowers can be used
in salads.

Service berry/saskatoon
Amelanchier
Blueberry-type fruit, harvest
when dark purple.

Fuchsia berries *Fuchsia*
Flowers and fruit are edible;
for bigger fruits try the
variety 'Berry'.

Viola flowers *Viola*
Delicate flowers can be
added to salads or cakes.

Hostas *Hosta*
Shoots and young leaves
can be eaten; the former
are known as urui in
Japanese cuisine.

Hostas

Viola

WATER

Water for wildlife

Water brings life to a garden, both literally and metaphorically. Many species will benefit from whatever water you can provide (it needn't be a pond), and there is enormous pleasure to be derived from simply watching insects, birds, amphibians and mammals use it to drink, bathe, breed and live in.

Bird baths

A shallow, secure bowl of water in which birds can drink, preen and bathe helps them to regulate the oil levels in their feathers, which is essential for flying and insulation.

Change the water and clean the bath weekly to avoid any transmission of avian diseases. A stone in the middle, protruding from the water, helps insects to escape and provides a perch for them and the birds.

In winter, be sure to break or remove any ice covering a bird bath and top up the water daily.

Hoverfly lagoons

Hoverflies are enormously beneficial pollinators, and while some lay their eggs on plants (where the larvae will then predate on aphids), others need stagnant water. As grass clippings and leaves rot and breed bacteria the smell will attract the adult; when the eggs hatch the larvae feed on the bacteria. The larvae aren't the most attractive (they're known as 'rat-tailed maggots') but are nonetheless fascinating to watch wriggling around the lagoon using a snorkel-like appendage to breathe.

Bee drinkers

A windowsill water feature, drinkers provide essential drinking water for bees and other insects in hot weather. Fill a saucer or similar dish with stones, creating a mound in the centre, and add rainwater so that the topmost stones are above the water level. This enables the bees to land and take off from a dry perch, and the shallow water will not soak or drown them. Change the water daily, topping it up if it evaporates during the day.

Use any watertight container, such as an ice-cream tub or the bottom half of a large plastic milk bottle: it should hold about 1 litre (34fl oz) of water. Pack the bottom two-thirds with fresh grass clippings and pour over rainwater so they are completely submerged. Top with a layer of leaf litter. Insert five or six sticks around the edge of the container – the new larvae will use these to climb out of the lagoon and drop to the ground to pupate. Put the lagoon somewhere quiet, in long grass if possible, topping up the water and clippings and/or leaves if necessary.

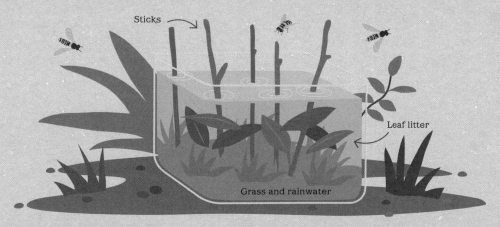

Sticks

Leaf litter

Grass and rainwater

Creating a pond

Water is one of the three essential ingredients to a successful wild garden, and the one component that will encourage the most life. The bigger a pond is, the more diverse the wildlife it will attract (a good size is at least 1 by 2m/3 by 6ft), but even sunken washing-up bowls can have a positive effect. One thing that will not help is fish, which will predate on the insects you hope to attract. The insects are the base of the pond food chain, and without them their predators (e.g. more insects, dragonflies, bats and birds) won't appear either. Keep fish ponds and wildlife ponds separate. For raised container ponds, see pages 74–75.

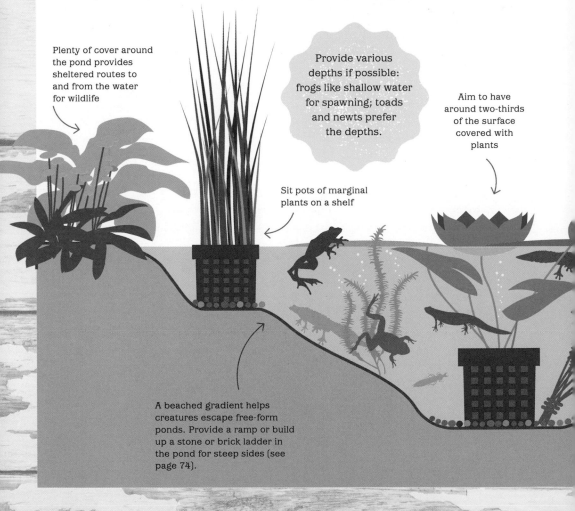

Plenty of cover around the pond provides sheltered routes to and from the water for wildlife

Provide various depths if possible: frogs like shallow water for spawning; toads and newts prefer the depths.

Aim to have around two-thirds of the surface covered with plants

Sit pots of marginal plants on a shelf

A beached gradient helps creatures escape free-form ponds. Provide a ramp or build up a stone or brick ladder in the pond for steep sides (see page 74).

A good mix of marginal, aquatic and oxygenating plants means there's no need for a pump, but a small fountain is fine for wildlife and helps keep the water clear.

Partial afternoon shade helps prevent evaporation and uncomfortable heat, but avoid building your pond too close to trees, or lots of leaves will fall in during autumn.

Shallow water supports the most life

Surround the pond with stones to weigh down and/or disguise the liner and allow wildlife to perch

To line the pond, puddled clay is the most natural option (see online tutorials), or use a thick plastic lining sheet. Alternatively, use a preformed hard plastic pond or repurpose a watertight container. Bed any liner on sand to avoid rips and cracks.

Making a pond wildlife-friendly

Having created a wonderful watery habitat, it's amazing how quickly life moves in to it. Make the surroundings just as appealing and sit back to enjoy the show.

Bog gardens

A useful additional habitat to the side of a pond, or a standalone feature, bog gardens will be popular with amphibians and insects. Partially shaded areas are best, to avoid any drying out. Simply dig out a patch of soil to a depth of 20–30cm (8–12in) and lay a sheet of pond liner into it. The aim is to retain some water but not all, so use a garden fork or similar to make holes in the liner. Alternatively, partially puddle some clay (see online tutorials). Put a layer of gravel in the base then add the soil back, mixed with plenty of leaf litter to help retain moisture, and add the plants.

Tips to help the wildlife in your pond

• Fill and top up the pond with rainwater if you can. If you use tap water, leave it for a week before adding the plants when filling. When topping up, leave the tap water to stand in a bucket for 48 hours before pouring it in gently.

• Always ensure there is at least one easy exit from the pond for all the creatures that will use it. Even amphibians will drown if they can't climb a slippery side. Several escape points on larger ponds means animals won't get exhausted and drown before they find an exit.

• Planting around the pond is useful to give cover from predators to baby amphibians and provide a sheltered route to the pond for other creatures.

• Don't be tempted to add spawn gathered from elsewhere as this can introduce pathogens.

• Shade the water with marginal plants, nearby trees and water lilies to avoid it getting too hot in summer. Shade some of the surroundings too, as froglets can get stuck on hot stones.

• Avoid too much plant matter falling into the pond, which can induce algae. Snip off dead stems and flower stalks of aquatic plants, and scoop or net fallen leaves off the surface.

• Break the ice every day in winter to keep the pond oxygenated.

• Pond plants can proliferate quickly – when removing any excess, leave them spread on the side of the pond for at least 24 hours to allow minibeasts within the plants to slide back into the water.

Provide resting places for wildlife

Plants for healthy ponds

Planting variety for healthy water

As with any planting, diverse leaf forms and flowering times will give the most interest and value to wildlife. Always choose reputable suppliers of pond plants to avoid inadvertently using invasive species (these can be checked against lists on government websites).

Pond plants

To keep the water healthy, plant a mix of marginals for shallow water, aquatics for deeper water and oxygenating plants. Use around six plants per square metre of water surface. See page 75 for small-pond plants.

Water crowfoot
Ranunculus aquatilis
Flowering, floating oxygenator with white buttercup-like flowers.

Starwort

Water starwort
Callitriche stagnalis
Floating oxygenator with pretty 'stars' of leaves on the water surface.

Water lily
Nymphaea species
Various sizes need different depths for their pots; pink or white flower options.

Frogbit

Frogbit
Hydrocharis morsus-ranae
Floating plant resembling a tiny water lily.

Pond sedge
Carex riparia
Marginal suited to larger ponds.

Dwarf bulrush
Typha minima
Marginal producing miniature versions of reed seedheads.

Hornwort

Hornwort
Ceratophyllum demersum
Floating oxygenator with dense foliage to shelter water wildlife.

Water lily

Dwarf bulrushes

Water mint

Water mint
Mentha aquatica
Flowering marginal with strongly scented edible leaves and flowers.

Blue flag
Iris versicolor
Marginal with purple/white flowers in summer.

Blue flag

Water avens

Bog plants

There are many plants that suit the water-logged soil of a bog garden, but these are especially popular with insects and relatively unfussy to grow.

Purple loosestrife
Lythrum salicaria
Tall spikes of purple flowers in summer.

Purple loosestrife

Marsh marigold
Caltha palustris
Clumps of leaves and yellow flowers in spring.

Marsh marigold

Water avens
Geum rivale
Clump forming, pink/orange flowers from spring to early summer.

Candelabra primroses *Primula* Candelabra hybrids
Flowers are borne in spring on tall spikes from a base rosette of leaves.

Yellow flag *Iris pseudacorus*
Tall leaves and spikes of yellow flowers in spring; for larger spaces.

Yellow flag

Gypsywort
Lycopus europaeus
Similar in appearance to nettles, with white flowers in late spring.

Shuttlecock fern
Matteuccia struthiopteris
No flowers, but clumps of fronds offer plenty of hiding places.

Shuttlecock fern

3

HELPFUL
HABITATS

A wild garden is, largely, a space in which the gardener is relatively hands-off, letting nature take its course. However, actively providing food and shelter can be a real benefit for wildlife that might otherwise be suffering. Research has shown that 30 different species of British birds have benefitted from a population boost as a result of garden feeding stations. The support from this food helps the birds not only survive the winter cold, but also gives them energy for growing, breeding and raising young. We can also put out boxes for bats and hedgehogs, and build homes for beetles, bees, slow worms and frogs, among many others. Most of these helpful habitats are unobtrusive and can be adapted to fit whatever size and style of garden you have. Making your garden a five-star wild hotel means visiting wildlife are more likely to become permanent residents, turning your garden into a backyard nature reserve.

Adding extra food to the garden

Birds and other wildlife come to know where they can access extra food, so it's important to commit to keeping a regular supply out all year round. Don't forget to also provide water to drink (see pages 114–115).

Bird feeders

Ensure feeders are kept clean by regularly washing them in hot soapy water – allow them to dry fully before refilling. Putting out several feeders to socially distance the birds, hanging feeders near other perching points and regularly changing the feeder locations can all help to prevent the spread of diseases such as the devastating *trichomonas* parasite.

Peanuts for birds Kibbled peanuts are an excellent energy-rich food for birds, but they must be intended for bird – not human – consumption. The peanuts should also be certified as having been found to be free from aflatoxin, a poisonous mould. Whole peanuts can choke young birds, so supply these in wire-mesh feeders that prevent the whole nut being taken at once.

From the many bird seed mixes available, it is worth investing in more expensive ones to avoid the grains used to bulk out cheaper versions. These grains are discarded by small birds and the waste can attract pigeons and rats, and germinate as weeds. Squirrels can be an annoying presence at bird feeders, but they are wildlife too; use a 'squirrel proof' feeder, or design an obstacle course to distract and divert them.

Good bird food choices

- Sunflower seeds/hearts
- Kibbled peanuts
- Maize (flaked)
- Nyger seeds
  (especially for finches and siskins)
- Suet balls and blocks (in winter; remove from net bags that can entangle wildlife)
- Mealworms (fresh or dried)
- Mild hard cheese, grated in small quantities
- Uncooked porridge oats
- Cooked rice
- Dried fruit (beware: sultanas and raisins are poisonous to dogs)

DON'T FEED TO BIRDS:

- Desiccated coconut
- Ultra-processed foods, sugary or salty foods
- Most dairy products
- Mouldy or stale food
- Cooking fat, margarine and similar products (soft fats smear on the birds, impeding flight and preening)
- Uncooked rice, lentils and peas (only larger species such as pigeons can digest these)
- Cooked porridge
- Dried dog/cat biscuits

A young robin feeds on mealworms

Feeding other wildlife

Most other wildlife will thrive in your garden if you have sufficient natural food for them. For example, planting flowers that are known to be popular caterpillar plants for moths will mean more food for bats, too. However, hedgehogs can be offered a poultry-based tinned cat or dog food or proprietary hedgehog biscuits, plus a saucer of water. Do not give them bread and milk – hedgehogs are lactose intolerant and this can kill them – and clean the bowls each morning.

Bird nesting boxes and materials

To tempt regular avian day-trippers into staying to rear a family, they'll need suitable nesting sites. Providing manmade bird boxes has the advantage that unobtrusive CCTV cameras can be incorporated to watch the nest and its inhabitants develop.

Bird boxes

It's possible to buy bird boxes in all styles and colours, but the birds are going to be more interested in security and homeliness, and a homemade option from untreated timber or woodcrete (a mix of sawdust and concrete) is just as good. Avoid boxes with perches and feeders attached as these enable predators.

Open-fronted boxes are favoured by robins and blackbirds. Closed boxes with an entrance hole can attract blue/coal/marsh tits (25mm/1in hole), great tits (28mm/1⅛in), sparrows and nuthatch (35mm/1⅜in) and starlings (45mm/1½in). Boxes for house sparrows and starlings, and specialised ones for swifts, can be fixed under roof eaves.

Between early autumn and mid-winter, clean out the box thoroughly, pouring boiling water over the empty box to kill parasites.

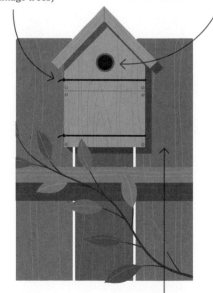

Face the box between northeast and southeast, not in full sun

Make sure boxes are sheltered from wind and rain

Fix securely with cable ties (screws and nails will damage trees)

Leave a clear approach for boxes with an entrance hole

Choose a quiet spot in the garden, where predators can't reach

Position 1.5–3m (5–10ft) off the ground

Nesting materials

In urban areas especially, birds might appreciate some help from a hanging buffet of different materials that they can use to build their nests, and it's interesting to watch which birds take what. Proprietary wire spirals are available into which the flyaway materials can be stuffed, or use a clean wire-mesh feeder. Other nesting materials can be tucked into the nooks between tree and bush branches, or gathered in small piles on the ground or other surfaces.

Dry leaves

Straw and dried grass

Dry moss, sheep's wool or short (5cm/2in or less) lengths of shredded paper

Short (5cm/2in or less), combed-out and chemical-free pet or human hair

What to avoid

• Long strands of anything (e.g. string, wool, hair)
• Plant or other material that might have been contaminated by pesticides, herbicides or other chemicals
• Damp materials that could rot or harbour fungus
• Tumble-dryer lint

Other materials to provide:
• Feathers
• Soft, downy plant material

Twigs

Bug hotels

Building a sheltered place for insects to live and perhaps lay their eggs is a great way to encourage them to the garden. It is possible to buy bee and bug hotels, but they are sometimes a case of style over substance, and it is very easy to make them at home instead, using untreated timber and natural materials.

A multipurpose bug hotel

Beetles, woodlice, lacewing flies, spiders and even amphibians and hedgehogs might check in to a hotel of this type, which is easy to create and is kept on the ground.

| Collect a variety of natural materials such as dry twigs, straw and hay, engineering bricks (those with holes through them), broken terracotta pots, dry leaves, lengths of dried hollow plant stems and/ or bamboo canes, and blocks of wood drilled with holes of a variety of sizes (3–10mm/⅛–⅜in). Avoid pine cones, which can open and close with changing humidity and potentially squash eggs laid within them.

Clumps of the same material will provide plenty of 'rooms' to explore

2 Create a frame for these materials using stacked pallets, an old wooden box or whatever is available.

3 Keep materials of the same type together in clumps, and ensure there's space at the base for amphibians to get in and out.

4 Cover the top with roof tiles, planks covered with roofing felt or even a green roof of turf and wildflowers – anything to reduce the amount of rain getting down into the layers.

5 In late summer, clear out the hotel and replace the materials with fresh ones to avoid a build-up of parasites and diseases.

A firebug visits an insect hotel

A variety of materials will attract a variety of bugs

Bee hotels

Hotels for solitary bees (and wasps) can be made easily from cardboard tubes of varying diameters (buy online, see page 140) housed within an open-fronted box with a back. Make the sides longer than the tubes to give them some shelter and mount on a fence or wall in an open, sunny spot.

Take the hotel down in mid-autumn and house it in a shed or somewhere similarly cool and dry to protect the grubs from birds over winter. Put it back out in spring to allow the baby bees to hatch and fly away, replace the tubes and clean the box with boiling water to kill harmful parasites and mites.

Bumblebees
Nesting in the ground or sometimes in bird boxes, bumblebees are notoriously fussy about their sites. Focus on offering plenty of food for them, and allow them to choose their own nesting spots within the garden.

Bat boxes

The best way to help bats is to create a wild garden rich in flowers and water that attracts night-flying insects that will be food for the bats. In addition, not using artificial exterior lighting and keeping cats indoors overnight will protect bats.

Fixed, waterproof roof. It is illegal to open a box once it is sited

Draught-free box of untreated timber

Opening at the base of 15–20mm (⅝–¾in) so that larger predators can't enter

A 'bat ladder' at the base gives the bats something to land on and crawl up

Bats like to roost in existing structures such as trees (alive or dead), buildings and underground sites, choosing different spaces through the year for hibernation and maternity roosts. It might take several years for bats to move into a roosting box, but once a bat box has been put up, it can only legally be checked or moved by a licensed bat worker.

Bat boxes can be purchased in a variety of designs, or make one using woodcrete or untreated timber. Put the box in a south-facing spot at least 3m (10ft) from the ground.

Log piles and dead hedges

Decaying wood can be a rich and diverse habitat of fungi, beetles, insects, spiders, centipedes and millipedes, and detritivores such as slugs. Hundreds of beetle species depend on dead wood, including the endangered stag beetle, and queen wasps will overwinter in log piles. The presence of so many other minibeasts attracts their predators, such as toads, newts, birds and slow worms.

Log pile

Pack soil between the logs

50cm/20in beneath the soil

2 The minibeasts won't care if your log pile is aesthetically pleasing or not, but to make a garden feature of it, cut logs to the same length and arrange them neatly, burying the base layer in the soil.

Uprights stop the pile collapsing

1 Site the pile somewhere relatively shady – too much sun will dry out the wood and not allow fungi and lichen to take hold.

Some buried logs

3 If desired, grow a scrambling climber over the top of your log pile to help it blend into the garden.

Beetle den

Stumps left to decay in the ground when a tree is felled form an important habitat – a single stump can play host to up to 400 species of beetle – and part of the ecosystem. If this isn't possible, create a vertical log pile by 'planting' a group of logs of varying sizes vertically. Smaller spaces could create a beetle den at the back of a border.

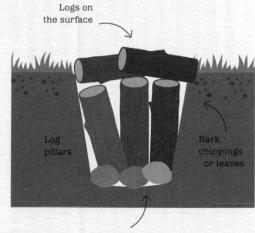

Logs on the surface

Log pillars

Bark chippings or leaves

Large stones

Logs from broadleaved trees (hardwood) will last longer than conifer softwood, so use mostly hardwood for your log pile if possible.

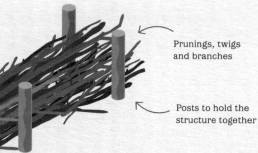

Prunings, twigs and branches

Posts to hold the structure together

30cm+ (12in+) between posts

Dead hedges

A useful habitat for insects and spiders, as well as a sheltered corridor for wildlife to move along, a dead hedge is branches and prunings pushed into a hedge shape between pairs of upright posts. The more neatly they are arranged, the better it will look, although birds might pull bits out as they scavenge for nesting material. Fungi will start to break down the material at the base, and more can be added to the top over time.

Rockeries and amphibian dens

Tortoiseshell butterfly

Rockeries — the old-style garden feature that is often largely stones and gravel — can be more beneficial for wildlife than their barren rocks would immediately suggest. The alpine plants that are generally used can provide early spring nectar for bumblebees and other insects, and their free-draining nature means spiders and other minibeasts that like to stay dry can find a home among the stones. A warm and sunny rock is also the ideal spot for insects and reptiles to bask. If you have such a feature and don't want to remove it, ensure it is as densely planted as possible, using scree-loving herbs such as marjoram, lavender, thyme and rosemary, which will be popular with bees, butterflies and hoverflies.

Building small cairns of stones in either sunny or shady places will provide shelter for many creatures. Sunny stones will be used as described above, but in the shade, the cool and damp spaces between the stones are ideal for many minibeasts and amphibians. Put them at the back of borders or near to water features, but ensure any stone piles are stable and sturdily constructed, so that they will not collapse on creatures moving about within them. Alternatively, bury the edges of a broken terracotta pot in the soil to create an arched den for frogs and toads — add some leaf litter for shelter and to attract their food species.

Reptile and amphibian hibernaculum

In winter, amphibians and reptiles go into a state of torpor to preserve energy, sleeping through the season in a warm and humid place. This can often be the compost heap, so creating a hibernaculum – a winter home – offers an alternative out of harm's way.

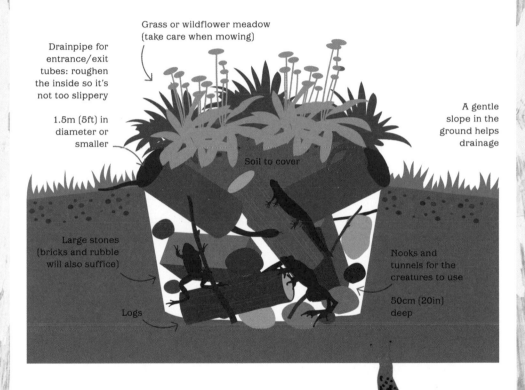

Grass or wildflower meadow (take care when mowing)

Drainpipe for entrance/exit tubes: roughen the inside so it's not too slippery

1.5m (5ft) in diameter or smaller

Soil to cover

A gentle slope in the ground helps drainage

Large stones (bricks and rubble will also suffice)

Nooks and tunnels for the creatures to use

50cm (20in) deep

Logs

Where do frogs live? Although all amphibians will mate and spawn in water, they spend most of their time on land in the damp and undisturbed corners of the garden. They like to hunt their food (e.g. slugs and worms) in the leaf litter and top layers of the soil and will shelter there and under stones.

Monitoring garden wildlife

Identify and record wildlife

FIELD GUIDE

For many, simply lazing in a deckchair and enjoying the butterflies, bees and birdsong is the greatest pleasure a wildlife garden can bring. However, it can be interesting – and a brilliant way to engage children in the garden – to seek out and observe its fauna in more detail. Identifying the creatures you find, using a field guide, is the first step, but if you want to encourage a particular type of wildlife, or help national efforts to bring species back from the brink, you will also need to record your results.

Some wildlife organisations have specific campaigns and/or recording days when they ask the public to become citizen scientists and to log what they see on a website or app. The data that such logging creates is of enormous value to scientists plotting different species' population decline, expansion and migration, and how the species are responding to various external factors such as urbanisation and climate change. These observations ultimately end up informing new or better ways to help the wildlife with which we share our world.

How to find out what is visiting your garden

The most powerful tool at any naturalist's disposal is patience. Sitting quietly and watching, as the wildlife gets used to your presence, is the best way to start. Do this regularly, as well as taking notice of the creatures around you as you work in the garden, and you will soon build up a picture of the creatures using your plot. Repeating observations regularly and recording them in a notebook or spreadsheet means you can see how the garden becomes more diverse over time. Remember to be extremely careful handling any trapped insects and to release them back to where they were found.

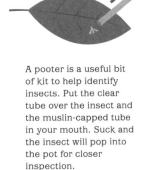

A pooter is a useful bit of kit to help identify insects. Put the clear tube over the insect and the muslin-capped tube in your mouth. Suck and the insect will pop into the pot for closer inspection.

Pooter

Bird nesting box cameras provide a live feed on the progress of the brood.

Trail cameras are another useful tool to identify nocturnal visitors – a motion sensor triggers recording and the footage can be checked later.

Trail camera

A moth trap is a great way to establish what is flying around at night. A lit box attracts the moths which, once in it, cannot escape until released the next day. Make your own simple version with a sheet, washing line and torch.

Moth trap

Glossary

Amphibian Cold-blooded animal that can breathe in air and water; frogs, toads and newts.

Annual plants Plant that grows from a seed, flowers, sets seed and dies within a single year.

Atmospheric carbon The carbon dioxide gas in the air around the planet. Levels of atmospheric carbon dioxide have risen sharply in recent decades, accelerated by human activity.

Bare root A plant, usually trees and shrubs during autumn and winter, sold without any soil around its roots.

Biennials Seed sown in summer will grow leaves but not flower until the following spring or summer.

Biodiversity Variety of plant and animal life.

Bulbs Plants such as daffodils grow foliage and flowers each year from an underground fleshy root that remains in the soil.

Detritivores Creatures that eat dead plant material, helping to turn it back into soil.

Diurnal Awake in the daytime, opposite of nocturnal.

Ecosystem Interacting community of plants and animals in a particular place. Can be large (the garden) or smaller sub-ecosystems (the log pile in the garden).

Fauna Animals of a certain area (as opposed to plants, which are described as the area's flora).

Floriferous Bearing many flowers.

Food chain Series of plants and organisms/animals each dependent on the next as its source of food, e.g. plant – aphid – ladybird – bird. Food chains interconnect into a food web.

Glaucous Grey-blue-green in colour.

Green manure (also called a cover crop) Plants sown into soil that won't be used for a while, often over winter, to prevent soil erosion and nutrient loss and/or add nutrients to the soil.

Habitat Natural environment or place to live for an animal or plant.

Insect Invertebrate creature with six legs and a body consisting of a head, thorax and abdomen; for example, beetles, ants and bees. May or may not have wings.

Invertebrate Animal without a backbone, including insects and creatures such as slugs, spiders and centipedes.

Larva/larvae (singular/plural) Caterpillar or grub stage of an insect's life. Eggs hatch into larvae (which differ significantly in appearance to the adult). Larvae pupate in order to metamorphose into the adult.

Larval food plant Plant on which an adult insect lays eggs so that when the eggs hatch the larvae can eat the plant. Some insects need specific plants for their larvae.

Leaf litter Layer of fallen leaves on a border or lawn that has started to decompose.

Mammal Warm-blooded animals that give birth to live young, such as shrews and hedgehogs.

Marginal An aquatic or bog plant that grows on the edges of ponds and in saturated soil.

Mulch Layer of organic matter such as compost, leafmould or bark chippings, or inorganic matter such as gravel, spread over a flowerbed. Functions include improving soil fertility and structure, moisture retention and weed suppression.

Nectar Sugar water from flowers, a syrupy substance that gives insects energy; important to insects, but the quality and relative levels in different flowers varies.

No-dig Method of growing, particularly edible plants, that involves minimal soil disturbance and regular mulching.

Perennials Plants that grow year after year. The foliage and flowers (top growth) of herbaceous perennials dies down in the autumn and sprouts anew in the spring.

Pollen The part of a flower needed for fertilisation; a protein-rich food for insects.

Pollination/pollinating Fertilisation of a flower by introducing pollen to the egg.

Reptile Cold-blooded creature with scaly skin, such as grass snakes and lizards.

Rootstock The roots and short section of a trunk, usually of a fruit tree, onto which another tree is grown. Different rootstocks confer qualities such as increased or reduced vigour and disease resistance onto the tree grafted to it.

Further resources

Books

RHS How Can I Help Hedgehogs?
Helen Bostock and Sophie Collins
(Mitchell Beazley, 2019)

RHS Do Bees Need Weeds?
Gareth Richards and Holly Farrell
(Mitchell Beazley, 2020)

Wildlife Gardening for Everyone and Everything
Kate Bradbury
(Bloomsbury, 2019)

RHS How to Create a Wildlife Pond
Kate Bradbury
(Dorling Kindersley, 2021)

RHS Get Growing: A family guide to gardening indoors and out
Holly Farrell
(Frances Lincoln, 2020)

Organic Gardening the Natural, No-dig Way
Charles Dowding
(Green Books, 2013)

RHS How to Garden the Low-Carbon Way
Sally Nex
(Dorling Kindersley, 2021)

Wildlife of a Garden: A thirty-year study
Jennifer Owen
(RHS, 2010)

Websites

rhs.org.uk
The Royal Horticultural Society. Extensive gardening information and advice; Plant Selector searchable database; campaigns such as Greening Grey Britain to help with alternatives to paved front gardens; Plants for Pollinators list.

wildlifetrusts.org
The Wildlife Trusts (UK national groups, links to county sub-groups); gardening for wildlife advice and information on local species.

ptes.org
The People's Trust for Endangered Species; information and stag beetle mapping citizen science project.

bats.org.uk
The Bat Conservation Trust and National Bat Helpline.

masonbees.co.uk
For bee nesting tubes to put into bee hotels.

Wildlife and conservation charities

There are a number of specialist charities that focus on helping particular wildlife, and they can be a good source of resources and specific advice as well as providing an opportunity to get involved in citizen science research projects, to provide vital data to scientists, and volunteering to help at local sites. An online search will reveal local and national groups, but here are some examples:

Royal Society for the Protection of Birds (RSPB)

Butterfly Conservation

Bumblebee Conservation Trust

Buzz Club (join nationwide research on hoverfly lagoons)

Froglife

Acknowledgements

My heartfelt thanks to all that worked on this brilliant book – may your gardens be always buzzing! I couldn't write without the patient support and encouragement of my wonderful husband: thank you, Kevin. Felicity, thank you for your enthusiasm and help; I hope you always find space for the wild in your life.

Index

Image credits

T = top; M = middle; B = bottom; L = left; R = right

Alamy
50 Kay Roxby; 99 M & J Bloomfield BR

Dreamstime
66L © Kevin Woodrow | Dreamstime.com

iStock
11 agustavop; 15B Mickis-Fotowelt; 16–17 sanddebeautheil; 24 mtreasure; 35T Deep Pixel; 38 Patrick Daxenbichler; 77 mtreasure; 84B whitemay; 104T cjp; 114B skhoward; 115 BecCreeper; 118 BasieB; 125T ian600f; 129T hsvrs; 130B hsvrs; 134T Richard Heath

Shutterstock
12 OksanaNizienko; 13T Hajakely; 13B Anatoliy Eremin; 14 Antonina Potapenko; 15T Andrew E Gardner; 16 PrestonPlucknett; 17 Richard P Long; 18 Irene Fox; 19T Chrislofotos; 19B Andi111; 20T Lorithie; 20B Hana Kolarova; 21 stimalan; 22 AVN Photo Lab; 23 ju_see; 24–25 Gardens by Design; 25 kzww; 26 Konstantin Aksenov; 27T simm49; 27B Peter Turner Photography; 28 Aleksandra Madejska; 29 Creatus; 30R Szasz-Fabian Jozsef; 30B PRILL; 31T Tamara Kulikova; 31M Per-Boge; 32T Anelovski; 32B Jamie Hooper; 33 Graham Corney; 34 Jeanette Dietl; 35B Hannamariah; 36 Cheng Wei; 37 Charise Wilson; 40L Jurga Jot; 40R Anna Kucherova; 41 Anne Elizabeth Mitchell; 42 Peter Turner Photography; 43T Peter Wey; 43B Artush; 44TL Peter Zijlstra; 44TR LecartPhotos; 44BL Jordon Sharp; 44BR Becky Stares; 45TL Martin Hibberd; 45TR emi; 45BL Coatesy; 45BR Anna Maria Louise Holm; 46TL Dolores M. Harvey; 46TR Jamieuk; 46M Keith Hider; 46BL antonella.lussardi; 46BR Denis Vesely; 47TR anat chant; 47ML Edwin Butter; 47M HWall; 47MR MagicBones; 47B cherryblossom; 48TL tchara; 48TR irin-k; 48BL Coatesy; 48BR artmandave; 49TL Subbotina Anna; 49TR anat chant; 49ML Fun_water; 49BL Eric Isselee; 49BR ATTILA Barsan; 52 Rod Williams; 53T Arsenio Keilin; 53B Judith Andrews; 54T Kollawat Somsri; 54BL Scisetti Alfio; 54BM Petr Salinger; 54BR Sopha Changaroon; 55TL Natalka De; 55BL Miguel AF55BM unpict; 55R Yulia_B; 56TL Rhoenbergfoto; 56TM SakSa; 56TR Sergey V Kalyakin; 56M Scisetti Alfio; 56BL weha; 56BM Alex Manders; 56BR Nadezhda Nesterova; 57L Arc Rajtar; 57M Nadezhda Kharitonova; 57TR Nick Pecker; 57LR StockPictureGarden; 58L Wagner Campelo; 58TR Olaf Simon; 58BR Southern Wind; 59TM Yu Zhang; 59TR Doubleclix; 59BL vandycan; 59BR Sandra Standbridge; 60L Angel Simon; 60M lenic; 60BM Scisetti Alfio; 60MR TravelerFL; 60BR Stefan_Sutka; 61L l Wei Huang; 61TM AN NGUYEN; 61M Sashko; 61TR Drop of Light; 61BR Marinodenisenko; 62 fotolinchen; 63TL Flower_Garden; 63ML cynoclub; 63BL Heriberto Forero; 63MT Epic Life Flashaes; 63MB JONG 16899; 63TR Anna Kvurt; 63BR M. Schuppich; 64L Lobanov Yury; 65TL Studio Light and Shade; 65TR Peter Turner Photography; 67TL Africa Studio; 67BL Grace Media; 67TR Ohhlanla; 67BR Khalangot Sergey L; 68 Franz Peter Rudolf; 69 1000 Words; 70TL oksana2010; 70BL StockPictureGarden; 70TM iava777; 70BM mamesuke; 70TR oksana2010; 70MR Vilor; 70BR Vic and Julie Pigula; 71TL Lopatin Anton; 71ML Nataly Studio; 71BL Robert Biedermann; 71TM Michael C. Gray; 71MM Richard Griffin; 71BM Sutorius; 71TR Henrik Larsson; 71MR Alan B. Schroeder; 71BR Kelly Whalley; 72 Chiara Zeni Photography; 73L VadimZosimov; 73R AngieC333; 75TL kristof lauwers; 75M lantapix; 75TR Kendo Nice; 75BR Martin Fowler; 76T Anna-Nas; 76B Maria Danilkina; 78L spline_x; 78M Gheorghe Mindru; 78R kristof lauwers; 79TL Mr. Meijer; 79BL Gabriela Beres; 79M Anastasiia Malinich; 79BR WildMedia; 80TL Funtay; 80BL Olga Shum; 80M Kuttelvaserova Stuchelova; 80TR ok_fotoday; 80TL Whiteaster; 81T prambuwesas; 81M Danita Delimont; 81B HHelene; 82L Elena11; 82R Sarah Marchant; 83T eurobanks; 83B A. Kiro; 84T Carmen Hauser; 85 terra-ferae-photography; 86L AndyNewman; 86TM Olexandr Panchenko; 86BM KYevhenii; 86TR David G. Boal; 86BR SabOlga; 87TL Przemyslaw Muszynski; 87BL M. Schuppich; 87TM Oksana Shevchenko; 87BM photogal; 87TR osoznanie.jizni; 87BR ezjay; 88L Liubov Isaeva; 88R chrisdorney; 89TL Natalia van D; 89BL Viki_tjdn; 89M Julia Lopatina; 89BM JIANG HONGYAN; 89TR Miti74; 89MR Kaichankava Larysa; 90 Rusana Krasteva; 91 Kolarova; 92T Alan Sau; 92B annikobyakova; 93 Miriam Doerr Martin Frommherz; 94 Richard Griffin; 95 Fanfo; 96 Elena Masiutkina; 97TL Sodel Vladyslav; 97BL Robert Lessmann; 97TM Olya Maximenko; 97BM FineShine; 97TR Robert Wilton; 97BR nnattalli; 98L Levon Avagyan; 98TR De Jongh Photography; 98BR Nanna Strandgaard; 99TL Nataly Studio; 99MR iztverichka; 99BL Snowbelle; 99M Sunbunny Studio; 99BM Wakhron; 99TR Ksenia Lada; 101 ChBsc; 103T ARTEM VOROPAI; 103M Scisetti Alfio; 103BM Roman Pelesh; 103R Le Do; 104B Masayuki; 105R P.S.Virk; 105B Danny Hummel; 106M Vilor; 106R nnattalli; 107T matteo sani; 107BL NIKCOA; 107BR suthas ongsiri; 108TL Carmen Hauser; 108M c_WaldWiese; 108BM Lubos Chlubny; 110 Nura M; 111 Kerry V. McQuaid; 112ML Fascinadora; 112BL Digihelion; 112TR nadia_if; 112MR Boida Anatolii; 113L Heri Afrilianto Manalu; 113TM Nella; 113M SaGa Studio; 113B Scisetti Alfio; 113R vladdon; 114T Christine Kuchem; 119T Alzay; 119B Fotimageon; 120L Ivaschenko Roman; 120TM tamu1500; 120BM OLIINYK INNA; 120TR Toni Genes; 120BR Oleksandr Lytvynenko; 121TL agatchen; 121ML wjarek; 121BL Natalia Baran; 121TM delyrie; 121BM Ivan Protsiuk; 121TR Stephen B. Goodwin; 121BR Heiti Paves; 122 Anouska13; 124L Ancha Chiangmai; 124R Konstantin Gushcha; 125B Coatesy; 128 Kristyna Henkeova; 128–129 Narine Avanesova; 129BR Uellue; 131L Jerome Whittingham; 131R gualtiero boffi; 134B Helen Pitt; 136T korkeng; 136L Butus; 136B sanddebeautheil; 142 irin-k